RAVES FOR JAMES PATTERSON

"NO ONE GETS THIS BIG WITHOUT AMAZING NATURAL STORYTELLING TALENT—WHICH IS WHAT JAMES PATTERSON HAS, IN SPADES."
—Lee Child

"THE MAN IS A MASTER OF HIS GENRE. WE FANS ALL HAVE ONE WISH FOR HIM: WRITE EVEN FASTER."
—Larry King, *USA Today*

"JAMES KNOWS HOW TO SELL THRILLS AND SUSPENSE IN CLEAR, UNWAVERING PROSE."
—*People*

"PATTERSON HAS MASTERED THE ART OF WRITING PAGE-TURNING BESTSELLERS."
—*Chicago Sun-Times*

"JAMES PATTERSON IS THE BOSS. END OF."
—Ian Rankin

"A MUST-READ AUTHOR...A MASTER OF THE CRAFT."
—*Providence Sunday Journal*

"THE PAGE-TURNINGEST AUTHOR IN THE GAME RIGHT NOW."
—*San Francisco Chronicle*

"PATTERSON IS A MASTER."
—*Toronto Globe and Mail*

For a complete list of books, visit JamesPatterson.com.

FILTHY RICH

THE JEFFREY EPSTEIN STORY

JAMES PATTERSON

JOHN CONNOLLY WITH TIM MALLOY

GRAND CENTRAL
PUBLISHING

NEW YORK   BOSTON

Grand Central Publishing
Hachette Book Group
1290 Avenue of the Americas, New York, NY 10104
grandcentralpublishing.com
twitter.com/grandcentralpub

Originally published in hardcover and ebook by Little, Brown & Company in October 2016
First oversize mass market edition: November 2017
Media tie-in oversize mass market edition: January 2020

Grand Central Publishing is a division of Hachette Book Group, Inc. The Grand Central Publishing name and logo is a trademark of Hachette Book Group, Inc.

The publisher is not responsible for websites (or their content) that are not owned by the publisher.

The Hachette Speakers Bureau provides a wide range of authors for speaking events. To find out more, go to www.hachettespeakersbureau.com or call (866) 376-6591.

ISBNs: 978-1-5387-1865-0 (media tie-in oversize mass market), 978-1-5387-1864-3 (media tie-in trade paperback), 978-0-316-36245-0 (ebook)

Printed in the United States of America

OPM

10 9 8 7 6 5 4 3 2 1

Interviewer: "It's the Icarus story—someone who flies too close to the sun."

Jeffrey Epstein: "Did Icarus like massages?"

—New York City, 2007

INTRODUCTION TO THE 2020 EDITION

This is how we got here.

In his lifetime, Jeffrey Epstein was a collector: of money and information, of people and experiences. And homes—he was especially known for his opulent residences, located in the United States, France, and the US Virgin Islands, where he hosted gatherings of some of the most powerful—and powerless—people in the world.

Yet in the summer of 2019, uninvited guests descended en masse on numerous Epstein residences.

They were federal law enforcement.

On July 8, 2019, FBI agents broke down the towering double doors to Epstein's $77 million town house at 9 East 71st Street in New York City. On August 12, 2019, more than a dozen authorities in FBI jackets raided Little Saint James, the seventy-acre private island Epstein purchased for $7.95 million in 1998. On September 23, 2019, French police raided Epstein's $8.6 million apartment in Paris, near the Arc de Triomphe.

And in a different kind of violation, in the early morning hours of August 14, the white front gates at the Palm Beach house Epstein bought for $2.5 million in 1990 were covered in red graffiti. By noon, the scarlet scrawl had been removed; but the damage Jeffrey Epstein himself inflicted on the very same people he once hosted as guests in his homes will never be so easily wiped clean and continues to spiral in a seemingly boundless arc.

Until the summer of 2008, money manager Jeffrey Epstein, then age fifty-five, was accustomed to moving freely among his residences. He was on the private island he nicknamed "Little Saint Jeff's" (after himself) when he got the call from his lawyer to return to Florida to face eighteen months of prison time on two state charges of sex solicitation, one of them involving a minor girl.

In an interview with the *New York Times* published a week later on July 1, Epstein's reaction to the news was to equate himself with Jonathan Swift's satirical explorer, Gulliver, whose "playfulness" among the Lilliputians "had unintended consequences." Epstein stressed his likeness to Gulliver, a giant among the little people, by saying, "That is what happens with wealth. There are unexpected burdens as well as benefits."

Yet the financier seemed unprepared to give up his benefits even as he suffered some of those burdens in navigating his forthcoming incarceration at the Main Detention Center in the Sheriff's Headquarters Complex at 3228 Gun Club Road, less than five miles from Epstein's home on El Brillo Way.

Epstein began receiving special privileges. In a memo dated August 2008, Captain Mark Chamberlain wrote, "I am authorizing that his cell door be left unlocked and he will be given liberal access to the attorney room where a TV will be installed."

Although the detention center was the primary holding

facility for male prisoners awaiting trial or sentencing, seven miles to the west sat the Palm Beach County Stockade, the county sheriff's office's lower-security compound.

In an interview for the first edition of this book, longtime Palm Beach County Sheriff Ric Bradshaw said he separated Epstein from the general jail population because "I didn't want him to be killed in custody." Epstein spent one night in the jail infirmary, then was driven to the minimum-security Stockade, which housed drug addicts, prostitutes, and nonviolent criminals.

In February 2009, Epstein moved to effectively private rooms at the Stockade, within the infirmary. Most of his time was not spent at the Stockade at all, but in a work-release program that ran twelve hours per day, six days per week—and for which he paid the sheriff's office $128,136 to cover the costs of deputy supervision.

This work-release ostensibly took place at the nonprofit Florida Science Foundation in an office building at 250 Australia Avenue in West Palm Beach—a nonprofit that Epstein himself had established in early 2008, months before pleading guilty. (Assistant State's Attorney A. Marie Villafana wrote to the sheriff's office on December 11, 2008, to decry how this "foundation" had been expressly "created on the eve of Mr. Epstein's incarceration in order to provide him with a basis of seeking work release," but if she received a response, it was never made official.) The headquarters were also within easy walking distance from the offices of Epstein's attorney, Jack Goldberger, and less than four miles from his Palm Beach mansion. Epstein was in fact daily driven to his home (past an elementary school) where he was allowed to spend hours at a time in the same place where his alleged offenses took place.

Yet no action was taken. Daily, Epstein rode with his personal driver—a Russian man named Igor Zinoviev, who had previously worked as a fighter in mixed martial arts—while deputies followed in an unmarked car.

A deputy who monitored Epstein while on work release spoke anonymously to NBC's West Palm Beach affiliate, WPTV, describing Epstein's staff at the Florida Science Foundation, who he says accompanied Epstein to his home for daily two-hour lunch breaks. "It looked like twenty-year-old females, well-dressed business attire," he said, adding, "I thought that it was strange that, besides me, myself, and Mr. Epstein, we were the only males in the office."

Not until 2019 would Palm Beach County Sheriff Bradshaw draw fire for this extraordinary, unprecedented lenient work-release deal, when Florida state senator Lauren Book called for an outside investigation, and a lawsuit was filed on behalf of Kaitlyn Doe, one of these young staffers. The filing stated that Kaitlyn first met Epstein in New York when she was seventeen and was later flown down to Palm Beach to work at the Florida Science Foundation. In reality, the filing stated, she was repeatedly coerced into sexual acts at the nonprofit's headquarters, and noted that "Jeffrey Epstein, through his brazen and powerful organization, was quite literally able to commit federal sex trafficking offenses at his work release office, during his jail sentence."

The foundation was dissolved shortly after Epstein finished his time in jail.

On July 7, 2009, after serving thirteen months of his eighteen-month sentence, Epstein officially left the Palm Beach County correctional system the same way he entered it—by limo.

The final stage of his sentence was one year of house arrest at his nearly twelve-thousand-square-foot, waterfront Palm Beach mansion. Although he complied with the Florida state requirement that he register as a sex offender, he openly defied the travel restrictions, flying fourteen times to New York and five times to the Caribbean during the first nine months of the one-year term.

Frequently his destination was Little Saint James, his property in the US Virgin Islands—now referred to by locals, dozens of whom worked on Epstein's property, as "Orgy Island" and "Pedophile Island."

Epstein followed a predictable routine: he'd land his private plane at Cyril E. King Airport in St. Thomas, then board a helicopter to take him to his island heliport. And although he was listed in the island's sex offender registry, it didn't appear to have much impact; according to many eyewitnesses, he was consistently seen in the company of young girls even after his sex-crime convictions. "It was like he was flaunting it," one witness said. "But it was said that he always tipped really well, so everyone overlooked it."

The one place Epstein wasn't required to register as a sex offender was in New Mexico. In 1993, Epstein had purchased over a thousand acres of land south of Santa Fe, New Mexico, where he built a fifty-thousand-square-foot mansion and called it "Zorro Ranch."

In the early 2000s, Epstein had begun expressing an interest in a troubling subset of genetic engineering called "transhumanism," which seeks to augment humans with technology, and he told several people about plans to turn his place in New Mexico into a "baby ranch" where he could impregnate "20 women at a time," according to sources in the *New York Times*. Epstein also developed a fascination with the unproven postmortem practice of cryonics, telling one like-minded individual that "he wanted his head and penis to be frozen," though no evidence exists that he actively pursued this.

Back in New York, unlike in New Mexico, according

to state guidelines Epstein was required to register as a "level 3" sex offender. A level 3 classification means the offender is a "high risk of repeat offense and a threat to public safety exists." Even so, Epstein seemingly moved about without any restrictions whatsoever. Nor did he bother to attend his so-called mandatory check-in appointments with the New York authorities who were supposed to be kept apprised of his whereabouts.

It was as if he was untouchable.

By September 2009, not long after Epstein's release from the Palm Beach County correctional system, the details of his plea deal were becoming public.

Brad Edwards, an ambitious TV-ready South Florida personal injury lawyer, had started gathering an ever-growing number of alleged victims, most of whose cases had never come to light because of how they had been handled. For instance, scores of alleged victims from the South Florida area were never even informed that Epstein's lenient plea deal was being put together based on one case, which was a violation of law. Many of the victims were outraged at these revelations, but the local media gave it scant coverage.

The civil case Brad Edwards was building was based on the testimony of dozens of women and girls, some underaged at the time, who all said they had been abused at Epstein's home on El Brillo or had been taken to his Caribbean island. According to a private investigator hired by production company Radical Media for its documentary on the Epstein case, sixty girls from Royal Palm Beach Community High School (which, despite the ostentatious name, was a rural school where 72 percent of the student body was considered "economically disadvantaged") may have gone to his house.

Much of Epstein's post-incarceration time and millions in lawyers' fees were spent waging a legal battle against Edwards.

Epstein initially sued Brad Edwards in 2008, claiming that Edwards, who'd briefly worked for a convicted Ponzi schemer named Scott Rothstein, was somehow using his aggressive advocacy for Epstein's victims as a vehicle to profit from Rothstein's Ponzi scheme. Edwards, who charged that the suit was a form of intimidation against him because he represented Epstein's victims, countersued for malicious prosecution and won.

The trial ended abruptly, however, with Epstein—who was not present in court—admitting through his attorney that his lawsuit had indeed been "a tool for extortion" meant to intimidate Edwards.

Several of Epstein's alleged victims had been set to testify; by settling, Epstein cut off their opportunity to tell their stories in court.

In September 2010, according to the *New York Times* and the *New York Post*, movie and television publicist Peggy Siegal arranged for Jeffrey Epstein to join the star-studded Hamptons guest list for a screening of the film *Wall Street: Money Never Sleeps*, where he was "greeted warmly." Although it was his first such public occasion in two years, "nobody blinked [that] he was there."

Epstein hadn't exactly been in hiding since his incarceration. He was often seen with young girls near his Palm Beach house or dining out around town at spots like Café Boulud in the Brazilian Court Hotel or the SurfSide Diner.

Later that same fall, Epstein threw a party in honor of Prince Andrew, with Siegal arranging the VIP guest list. Her invitation—simply, "Do you want to have dinner with Prince Andrew?"—was enough to entice several wealthy and celebrity guests, including TV hosts Katie Couric, Charlie Rose, and George Stephanopoulos, to show up at Epstein's New York town house to meet the royal guest of honor. "That dinner was the first and last time I've seen him [Epstein]," Stephanopoulos later stated. "I should have done more due diligence. It was a mistake to go."

Over a decade earlier, in 1999, Epstein's Oxford-educated, British-socialite girlfriend, Ghislaine Maxwell, had used her connections to first introduce Epstein and Prince Andrew. Thereafter, Epstein had hosted the prince at several of his luxury homes—though "no more than only once or twice a year," according to Prince Andrew—and the prince had included Epstein as his guest at Windsor Castle to celebrate the birthday of his mother, Queen Elizabeth II, in 2000.

The visits continued even after Epstein's time in jail, as evidenced by both the dinner party and widely circulated photographs and video of Prince Andrew standing in the doorway of Epstein's New York town house in December 2010, plus photographs of the two men walking together in Central Park.

As the *New York Post* reported in September 2019, however, it was that coverage of Andrew's four-day trip to New York City which derailed the friendship between the two men (whom the *Post* labeled "the prince and the pervert"). The tabloid dig sparked a feud that brought to light a $24,000 debt owed to Epstein by Prince Andrew's ex-wife, Sarah Ferguson, who publicly decried Epstein's pedophilia, only to have Epstein threaten to sue for defamation.

Still, the royal's connection to Epstein lingered longer than that of the woman who'd first introduced them. Following Epstein's guilty plea in 2008, Ghislaine Maxwell,

Epstein's former girlfriend and alleged madam, markedly distanced herself from their long and complex relationship, though it's unclear exactly when they parted ways.

As part of the 2008 plea bargain, Maxwell, along with others who might have been coconspirators, had received immunity from any Florida-related charges. She denied ever engaging in sex with children or procuring girls, though there was widespread belief among Palm Beach law enforcement that she was a full accomplice, who orchestrated liaisons for Epstein in New York.

In 2012, Maxwell founded and headed the Terra-Mar Project, an environmental organization intended, according to its tax filings, "to create a global ocean community to give a voice to the least protected, most ignored part of our planet—the high seas." Yet Christopher Mason, a reporter and onetime friend of Maxwell's, told the *New York Times* that he "wondered if her primary motivation for starting the foundation was oceanic conservation or the conservation of Ghislaine Maxwell."

It was under the auspices of TerraMar that Maxwell traveled to a conference in Reykjavik, Iceland, in 2013 and met Scott Borgerson. Though Maxwell described Borgerson to friends as a "Navy SEAL," he was actually a retired officer in the Coast Guard and a former fellow for the Council on Foreign Relations, as well as chief executive of CargoMetrics Technologies.

In 2016, Borgerson purchased property in a secluded area of the wealthy Boston suburb Manchester-by-the-Sea, and in August 2019, the *Boston Globe* reported that neighbors had spotted Maxwell (who called herself "G" or "G Max") living in town over the previous years. Borgerson declined to corroborate the rumors, commenting only that "My private life is my private life."

Maxwell kept a very low profile. In April 2016, she sold her five-story town house at 116 East 65th Street in Manhattan—only blocks from Epstein's 71st Street residence—for a reduced asking price of $15 million (still a tidy profit from its $4.95 million purchase price in 2000), and thereafter her lawyers were evasive about their client's whereabouts, claiming she had no known address.

Until the *New York Post* printed a picture of the social-ite seated at an unlikely location—an outdoor table at a Los Angeles–area In-N-Out Burger—in August 2019, no photos of Maxwell in public had surfaced since 2016. But then a *Daily Mail* reporter turned up evidence that even that photo had been faked.

Maxwell was not a fugitive, but clearly law enforce-ment wanted to talk to her about what role she may have played in Epstein's alleged trafficking operation. And it seemed equally clear that she had no desire to do so.

In 2009, Epstein had settled with yet another accuser, Virginia Giuffre, who'd filed a civil complaint which alleged Epstein had not only sexually abused her from 1999 to 2002 but had also caused her to be abused by his "adult male peers, including royalty, politicians, acade-micians, businessmen, and/or other professional and personal acquaintances." Furthermore, she'd accused Ghislaine Maxwell of "assistance and participation" in these crimes, which Maxwell vigorously denied, calling Giuffre a liar—so in 2015, Giuffre filed a suit against Maxwell herself, for defamation.

The 2015 suit was settled in 2017, on the eve of when the trial was meant to occur. But in 2019, the *Miami Her-ald* successfully petitioned for the documents relating to that 2015 lawsuit to be unsealed—releasing "thousands of documents, incident reports, photos, flight logs, and more detailing the recruitment of young women and girls."

Among the dozens of disturbing stories of girls treated

as "sex slaves" that Giuffre's complaint detailed were those of twelve-year-old French triplets, whom Epstein flew to Florida as a "birthday present" to himself. "Jeffrey bragged after he met them that they were twelve years old and flown over from France because they're really poor over there and their parents needed the money or whatever the case is," Giuffre is quoted as saying.

A French prosecutor explained the process by which a person with knowledge of these events could give evidence without initial risk of criminal repercussions. "Prince Andrew would certainly be an obvious person to assist with this inquiry," the prosecuting source said. "He is clearly deeply involved in this case."

And surely many would like to know more about what one woman close to Maxwell recalled her saying of the underage victims: "They're nothing, these girls."

When former Miami US attorney Alexander Acosta was nominated to the post of US Secretary of Labor in June 2017, he briefly addressed questions during his confirmation hearing about the plea deal he'd approved for Jeffrey Epstein. While one lawmaker requested more records from the Epstein case, it went no further, and Acosta was confirmed.

But local media in Florida knew the story well. The *Miami Herald* began a scathing series of reports punctuated by interviews with Epstein victims that raised the question: How did US attorney Acosta let Epstein get away with this?

Acosta tossed the blame for Epstein's light sentence back on Barry Krischer, the state attorney in Palm Beach County, suggesting that Krischer "was ready to let Epstein walk free, no jail time, nothing," while he, Acosta, had done all he could do given the legal circumstances.

Krischer responded in kind. From his home in the Florida Keys, Krischer lambasted Acosta in an e-mail sent to media, writing, "Mr. Acosta's recollection of this matter is completely wrong" and he "should not be allowed to rewrite history."

Regardless, local and federal law enforcement had clearly dropped the ball. Despite significant evidence that Epstein was running an industrial-scale child trafficking and molestation operation, both state and federal prosecutors had merely slapped him on the wrist and sent him on his way.

Arguably the one member of law enforcement who'd chased after Epstein the hardest was Joseph Recarey, a Queens-born Palm Beach police detective who led the Epstein investigation in Florida. Recarey, one of the most decorated police officers in the history of the department, died unexpectedly on May 25, 2018, at fifty years old. The Palm Beach Police Department took the news hard. Said one officer of Recarey, who'd delicately and skillfully taken the video depositions from Epstein's victims, "He made the case against Epstein. It was grueling and he never got to see justice done."

In a baffling move, Jeffrey Epstein decided to memorialize his time behind bars with a prison-themed mural on the second floor of his New York town house. According to publicist R. Couri Hay, Epstein proudly showed off the painting, pointing to a likeness of himself flanked by guards and surrounded by barbed wire and telling Hay, "That's me, and I had this painted because there is always the possibility that could be me again."

Hay, who had a reputation for helping rehabilitate tarnished images, met with Epstein on a handful of occasions after his incarceration but never officially signed the disgraced financier on as a client. "I don't want 'billionaire pervert' to be the first line of my obituary," Epstein told him. But Hay, who last met with Epstein about three weeks before his 2019 arrest, said he felt Epstein "was in denial" about the seriousness of his situation. It was obvious that while Epstein was "clearly guilty," he still "wasn't ready to make amends," Hay said. Instead of atoning for his crimes, Epstein downplayed them, scoffing that the "pedophile" label was inaccurate considering that girls he'd been with were "tweens and teens."

Hay offered Epstein a number of potential pathways to public redemption, while also pointing out, "I told Jeffrey the only person who could forgive him is God." Ultimately, Hay told the *New York Post* on July 16, 2019, "I could have told him to commit suicide but that wouldn't have been very constructive."

Around the time of Epstein's last meeting with Hay, he also made his last visit to the island of Little Saint James. According to accuser Sarah Ransome, Epstein's behavior there was becoming increasingly depraved, to the point that she undertook a risky escape. "I had been raped three times that day," Ransome told the British newspaper the *Telegraph*. But a surveillance camera captured her fleeing Epstein's property by bike, and Epstein thwarted her plan to swim the several miles distance from the island to St. Thomas. "A shark would have been my best friend at that point," she said.

There is no true refuge for a convicted pedophile, but to Epstein, France, with its byzantine extradition laws and no legal minimum age of consent, might have seemed like a safe haven.

In mid-June 2019, he flew east across the Atlantic for a three-week stay at the apartment he owned on Paris's

Avenue Foch. The place had a view of the Arc de Triomphe, where the 16th, 17th, and 8th arrondissements meet, and Paris beckoned, despite Epstein's increasing legal jeopardy in the US.

In February 2019, the Department of Justice had opened an investigation into federal prosecutors' handling of Epstein's plea deal, and the Southern District of New York was mounting a sex-trafficking case with new victims since the Florida conviction.

On July 6, at Paris-Le Bourget Airport, Jeffrey Epstein boarded his private plane en route to Teterboro, New Jersey. The FBI was waiting.

In a September 21, 2019, interview with *Dateline* NBC, former Palm Beach police chief Michael Reiter posits that back in 2005, Epstein may have been tipped off by a mole in the department before the raid that resulted in the financier's 2008 conviction.

That time, there were signs pointing to a hasty cleanup. For instance, "All the wires were left hanging there," Reiter says of a missing video surveillance computer that may have contained further incriminating evidence.

In 2019, there were no leaks.

Upon disembarking the plane on July 6, 2019, Jeffrey Epstein was handcuffed and taken to the Metropolitan Correctional Center, which has housed such notorious prisoners as drug lord Joaquín "El Chapo" Guzmán Loera, Ponzi schemer Bernard Madoff, and mob boss John Gotti.

Whereas in the Palm Beach County prison, sheriff's deputies had addressed him as "the client," "Mr. Epstein," or even "Jeffrey," he was now inmate 76318-054. The wealthy man accustomed to every creature comfort now found himself housed in a damp cell crawling with vermin.

As one of Epstein's many lawyers Mariel Colón Miró, twenty-six, whose first client had been Mexican drug lord "El Chapo" (Epstein was her second), described the Metropolitan Correctional Center, "It is not a sanitary place. You can see rats walking around. It is nasty."

It was later revealed that Epstein requested long periods of counsel with Miró and his other attorneys in the visiting areas and available meeting rooms, all in an attempt to escape the confinement of his cell. In an abrupt departure from the treatment Epstein received during his Florida incarceration, the door of his cell at the Metropolitan Correctional Center was never left unlocked.

The indictment issued by US attorney Geoffrey Berman stated that Jeffrey Epstein "created a vast network of underage victims for him to sexually exploit." If convicted of federal sex-trafficking and conspiracy charges, Epstein now faced a maximum forty-five-year sentence, which would likely amount to a life sentence given his age of sixty-six.

At a July 7, 2019, news conference, Berman revealed that a search of Epstein's New York town house had uncovered photos of underage girls, and a safe seized by the feds contained $70,000 in cash, nearly fifty diamonds, and a falsified passport.

Twelve days after being arrested, Epstein was denied bail.

Fallout for Epstein associates came quickly and severely.

Retail billionaire Leslie Wexner, eighty-one, had first met Jeffrey Epstein in the mid-1980s through Robert Meister, a former insurance executive at Aon. Sandy

Lewis, the money manager and Wexner confidant whom Epstein replaced, said Wexner is "a shy man who got taken" during his fifteen-year association with Epstein, which ended in 2007.

On August 7, 2019, Wexner issued a statement that revealed the extent of the damages that occurred to him at Epstein's hands when Wexner, then the chairman of L Brands (which included Victoria's Secret and Bath & Body Works), allowed Epstein access to his family's investments and trusts. In 1989, through a corporation under the dual control of both men, Epstein purchased his town house at 9 East 71st Street from Wexner for $13 million. In 1991, Wexner granted Epstein power of attorney, and, according to Wexner, "he had wide latitude to act on my behalf with respect to my personal finances," a decision which allowed Epstein to misappropriate "vast sums of money," including a single $46-million transfer. "I am embarrassed that, like so many others, I was deceived by Epstein," Wexner wrote. "I deeply regret having ever crossed his path."

Publicist Peggy Siegal said in an interview with the *New York Times* published on July 13, 2019, that her "relationship with Mr. Epstein was not a paid one," yet in a profile published less than a week later on July 19, her statement was quickly upended by a staffer telling the *Hollywood Reporter* that the two spoke frequently, and that since Epstein "wanted to go to every party," he would provide expensive gifts and travel reimbursement in exchange for entry to events.

It was further revealed that Siegal bent studio rules regarding preapproved guest lists to allow Epstein to attend without her clients' knowledge. As recently as March 2016, Siegal had arranged for Epstein to attend the New York premiere of the Warner Bros. film *Batman v Superman: Dawn of Justice*.

In July 2019, Siegal lost major clients, including Netflix, FX, and Annapurna Pictures, because of her association with Epstein.

"If you looked up Jeffrey Epstein online in 2012, you would see what we all saw," Leon Botstein, president of Bard College, told the *New York Times* in 2019. Although Epstein appeared to have some kind of a past, basically he "seemed like an ex-con who had done well on Wall Street."

Bard accepted $125,000 in unsolicited donations from Epstein, but the bulk of Epstein's financial contributions went to two famed institutions in Cambridge, Massachusetts: MIT and Harvard.

In a September 8, 2017, interview with *Science* magazine, Epstein said, "The MIT [Massachusetts Institute of Technology] Media Lab is a good example" of an institution he supported because "It's my natural bent to move toward the maverick and rebels who don't fit in."

Epstein may have been referring as much to the scientists as to Joichi Ito, at that time the Media Lab's director. A September 6, 2019, exposé in the *New Yorker* revealed that Ito maintained his relationship with Epstein, who made and orchestrated what totaled millions in donations to the lab—including money earmarked for investment funds under Ito's control—long after Epstein's 2008 conviction as a sex offender technically disqualified him from being a university donor. Ito—who had taken elaborate measures to ensure Epstein's donations remain anonymous—resigned the day after the exposé ran.

On September 12, 2019, MIT's president, L. Rafael Reif, also admitted in a statement circulated by e-mail that in 2012, during his early weeks leading the university, he had signed a donor thank-you letter to Epstein. The university is undergoing an independent investigation of its interactions with Epstein.

That same day, Harvard's president, Lawrence S. Bacow, e-mailed "A Message to the Community Regarding Jeffrey Epstein," corroborating reports in the *Chronicle of Higher Education*, the *New York Times*, and elsewhere that Epstein had given just under $9 million to Harvard between the early 1990s and 2007, and that the university would allocate the remaining unspent balance of $186,000 to support victims of human trafficking.

Bill Gates's troubles with Epstein began in 2014, when, according to Gates, Epstein "was introduced to me as somebody who could bring more people into philanthropy." On November 7, 2014, bgC3 (now Gates Ventures) awarded MIT Media Lab $2 million, adding to the letter, "Please note that Bill wishes to remain anonymous with this contribution." Nevertheless, in 2019, the *New Yorker*, Fox News, and Axios all traced the donation back to having been at Epstein's suggestion, to which Gates stated, "I wish I hadn't met with him."

Elon Musk was similarly burned when Epstein leaked sensitive conversations he said he'd had with Tesla's chief executive to *New York Times* reporter James Stewart around the time in 2018 when Musk was debating whether to take the luxury automaker he'd founded private. Though Stewart also printed Tesla's rebuttal ("It is incorrect to say that Epstein ever advised Elon on anything"), he ended the piece with the provocative question, "What might he [Epstein] have told me?"

What would soon be revealed were the more than two thousand documents released by federal prosecutors including affidavits and depositions of key witnesses from Virginia Giuffre's 2015 civil lawsuit against Jeffrey Epstein and his associate, Ghislaine Maxwell.

There would be no coming back from that.

* * *

Before July 2019, Nicholas Tartaglione (a former Briarcliff Manor, New York, police officer) was known—and feared—in certain circles as the accused killer of four men in a botched drug deal. He will now forever be linked to Jeffrey Epstein, his cellmate at Metropolitan Correctional Center.

On July 23, 2019, Epstein was found curled on the floor of their shared cell, semiconscious and with bruises on his neck. Epstein was put on suicide watch while prison officials investigated whether the injuries were self-inflicted or the result of an attack by Tartaglione.

Less than a week later, on July 29, Epstein was removed from the watch list. Assistant District Attorney Stephen Boyd later answered inquiries from the US House Committee on the Judiciary, explaining that it was "a doctoral-level psychologist who determined that a suicide watch was no longer warranted."

This latest order lessened the observation requirements on Epstein from constant by staff or "inmate companions" (in mid-August, Tartaglione was cleared in the July 23 incident) to staff checks at thirty-minute intervals.

According to a *New York Post* interview with a prison source, Epstein told his lawyers that "the cop [Tartaglione] roughed him up, and that's why they got him off suicide watch."

On the morning of August 10, 2019, as guards distributed breakfast to the inmates of 9 South, Epstein was found dead in his cell. His neck, constricted in a bedsheet, was broken.

The initial death certificate, filed on August 11—the same day the autopsy was performed—lists "Immediate Cause: Pending Further Study," launching what

Epstein lawyer Reid Weingarten termed "conspiracy theories galore." New York City's chief medical examiner, Barbara Sampson, effectively ended the discussion on August 16, explaining in her report that Epstein's broken neck bones were consistent with a hanging victim of Epstein's advancing age. The official cause of death was suicide.

On the overnight shift of August 9 into the tenth, the ratio of inmates to guards in the federal jail was 750:18, with two of those guards assigned to monitor Epstein on unit 9 South. Despite strict instructions against leaving Epstein alone in his cell, for a period of three hours, no thirty-minute checks were performed because, according to the Federal Bureau of Prisons, the guards had fallen asleep.

Many were outraged that Attorney General William Barr, whose responsibilities include overseeing the Federal Bureau of Prisons, failed to explain how Epstein was able to commit suicide while a prisoner in the high-security Manhattan correctional center. In an interview with NBC News, Cameron Lindsay, a former federal prison warden who supervised multiple facilities over the course of his career, said, "Gosh, if I were him [Epstein], I'd want to be dead and I'm sure there are a multitude of people that would have wanted him dead. It's corrections 101."

On August 13, the Federal Bureau of Prisons, citing Attorney General Barr's complaint of "serious irregularities at this facility," reassigned Metropolitan Correctional Center warden, Lamine N'Diaye, and put the two guards on leave. Barr was forced to admit to the press that of the fifteen MCC employees subpoenaed about the events surrounding Epstein's suicide, "unfortunately, there have been some delays because a number of the witnesses were not cooperative."

At a law enforcement conference in New Orleans, Louisiana, Barr turned his concern to Epstein's victims. "But let me assure you," he remarked, "that this case will continue on against anyone who was complicit with Epstein. Any coconspirators should not rest easy. The victims deserve justice and they will get it."

Among Epstein's accusers, there is pressing concern that Barr's promise will prove impossible to deliver. On August 27, US district judge Richard M. Berman presided over a highly unusual hearing. Dozens of women gathered in his courtroom that day to testify against an absent defendant, his indictment vacated upon a death Berman declared "a stunning turn of events."

Jennifer Araoz, who said that she was raped by Epstein as a fifteen-year-old high school student in New York, stated, "They let this man kill himself and kill the chance of justice for so many others in the process, taking away our ability to speak."

Two days before he died, Jeffrey Epstein laid one final trap. He drafted a twenty-one-page will, "hereby revoking all prior Wills and Codicils made by me," and directed it to be filed in St. Thomas. According to the *New York Post*, a Virgin Islands filing keeps the document "more private, because that is not where people would look. There is always a risk that [in New York] it would be leaked."

Though Jeffrey Epstein's brother, Mark, stood to inherit the estate valued at more than half a billion dollars had no will been filed, the August 8 document lists no direct beneficiary, only that all of Epstein's assets will flow into the newly created "1953 Trust," a possible reference to the year of Epstein's birth.

Any current and future petitioners against the estate now face an additional legal obstacle.

Palm Beach detective Joe Recarey described Epstein's operation as a "sexual pyramid scheme." Around one hundred women say they were victimized, and there are indications that the count could be even higher.

"He said he'd served his time and assured me that he changed his ways," publicist Peggy Siegal recalled.

A retired Palm Beach police detective who was involved in the original Florida investigation had a darker view on Epstein's potential for rehabilitation. When asked in 2014, five years after Epstein was released from prison, if he believed the convict was rehabilitated, the detective didn't hesitate to answer.

"He's still doing it," he said. "These guys never stop."

In crime writing, there is the first view and the long view.

What follows was originally published in 2016. Though allegations against Jeffrey Epstein had begun making headlines in Florida a decade earlier, his criminal case was not yet on the national radar. But we felt that it was a powerful story and one that needed to be told—here, in the first published book on the subject.

Even as this updated edition hits the shelves, the story continues to unfold in surprising and dramatic ways, making these pages a living archive of the case—you'll see many of the original police interviews and court documents are contained here, much of it in the unvarnished words of the young girls who were Epstein's victims.

"Clearly, the rich have the big advantage when they go to court," we told the *Wall Street Journal* in its coverage around the release of this book's first edition;

"Money can do a lot of things." That hasn't changed. But even Epstein wasn't ultimately able to buy his way out of the latest charges against him or silence his victims indefinitely.

We hope a timely telling of the earliest days of the criminal investigation somehow furthered that.

—James Patterson and Tim Malloy,
Palm Beach, September 25, 2019

AUTHOR'S NOTE TO THE 2016 EDITION

Late one afternoon, while taking a leisurely stroll on the Upper East Side of Manhattan, Tim Malloy, a friend of mine and a collaborator on this book, nearly ran into a trim, silver-haired neighbor of ours from Palm Beach.

The man was walking down Madison Avenue, and several things about him were striking. For one thing, he was wearing slippers. Expensive, embroidered, monogrammed slippers. But slippers all the same.

For another, he was accompanied by two attractive women. Even in Manhattan, an island that attracts beautiful women from all over the world, these women stood out.

As the man half shuffled, half walked down the avenue, the women walked slightly behind him, as if they were attendants or staff.

Tim followed, keeping a respectable distance, as the threesome made a right onto 71st Street and headed toward an enormous town house—a house that was almost a fortress—right in the middle of the block. The imposing residence had a stone facade and a fifteen-foot-high front door that wouldn't have looked out of place protecting a castle. And, like our neighbor's slippers, the house had a monogram: raised brass letters that spelled out JE.

The house and, quite possibly, the two women belonged to Jeffrey Epstein, a rich and powerful man who was also a registered sex offender with a strong taste for underage women.

Not just sixteen- and seventeen-year-olds. But younger girls as well.

Epstein was alleged to have abused dozens of young women, or, more accurately, girls. He'd settled potential lawsuits with some of them. He'd done a bit of prison time for his crimes. A *bit* of time. And now here he was, out in the world again.

Accompanied by two beautiful young women.

I had been hearing hair-raising stories about Jeffrey Epstein for a couple of years. Our interests could not have been more different, but Palm Beach, where we both live, is small and tightly knit, and we knew some of the same people.

Epstein's arrest had made headlines in papers all over the world. But in Palm Beach, it caused a scandal that continues to set off aftershocks and leave a bad smell.

So I had followed Epstein's case in the media and talked about it over dinners with friends. I wondered why it had taken so long for the Palm Beach police to catch up with Epstein. And, once they did, why he had served so little jail time.

Those were the obvious questions, but there were others: How had Epstein made his money, possibly billions? No one seemed to know. And while the news media had some details about the underage girls, reporters seemed only to know what had happened *at the moment of his arrest*.

Epstein definitely liked his massages. He got them from two, even three, young women a day, right in his mansion on the island. He'd been operating on an almost industrial scale. But who were these girls? Where had they come from? How did they find their way to his home on a secluded street in Palm Beach?

Epstein had powerful friends. He'd flown Bill Clinton around in his private jet and rubbed shoulders with heads of state, Nobel Prize winners, any number of billionaires. Prince Andrew, the man sixth in line to the British throne, had been a close friend.

Were any of these connections the reason that Epstein was now a free man?

I wanted to know. After all, our homes were a half mile apart, and Epstein's actions had had an undeniable impact on the town where I lived. Stirred by that sighting of Epstein up in New York, Tim Malloy and I began to investigate.

We partnered with John Connolly, a tough, no-nonsense journalist who had once been a cop with the NYPD and had been following the Epstein story for close to ten years.

Working together, we interviewed Epstein's friends, going all the way back to his childhood; we met with Epstein's acquaintances, employees, neighbors, and business associates, and finally with the families of his victims. We interviewed law enforcement officers who'd worked on the investigation in Palm Beach and lawyers on all sides of the resulting court cases, some of which are still working their way through the court system.

Combining our interview material with evidence obtained from court filings and other investigations, such as the one conducted by Connolly's *Vanity Fair* colleague Vicky Ward, we began to put the pieces together.

In a few instances, we have re-created brief scenes

and snatches of dialogue. These are based on interviews, police investigation documents, and court filings. We changed the names and identities of the girls, hoping to protect them from more embarrassment and harm.

There never was any doubt that Jeffrey Epstein was guilty. He admitted as much in the non-prosecution agreement he agreed to sign in 2007. The question is, what exactly was he guilty *of*?

This book attempts to answer that question and many others about this strange and mysterious man. These days people all around the world are angry about and suspicious of the super rich and powerful. The story of Jeffrey Epstein is an object lesson about why we ought to be. To put it simply, some people think they can operate outside the law. And that's what they do.

—James Patterson, Palm Beach, February 20, 2016

PART I
The Crime

CHAPTER I

Mary: February 2005

It's a typically slow South Florida Sunday, and Mary's staring into the mirror, trying to wipe the morning cobwebs away from her dark, sleepy eyes.

She's a pretty girl, tiny—just five feet three inches tall—but tanned and athletic, with curly black henna-streaked hair.* Her bedroom's a playland of pinks and pastels, stuffed animals, and boy-band posters. But Mary's a teenager now. Fourteen years old. She even has a boyfriend. He's cute and popular. Joe† is the heartthrob of her school, and Mary's feelings for him are new to her, powerful, hard to untangle. She's thinking of Joe as she presses the Play button on her iPod.

The MP3 player's on shuffle. There's no telling what song will come up, and Mary's head drops dramatically in anticipation. Then a loud, sexy throb spills out of the earbuds: Britney Spears. The bass line takes over, and

---

* Mary's name, some identifying details, and dialogue have been changed.

† Joe's name, some identifying details, and dialogue have been changed.

she starts to dance, moving her hips as she lip-synchs the lyrics:

With a taste of a poison paradise . . .

Mary's swept away by the song. She's twirling around and around, flinging her arms out to grab the clothes hanging up in her closet—*it's like embracing ten thousand fans!* Then she stops and pulls out the earbuds. Suddenly she's become fourteen again. Just a girl, jittery, nervous.

What she's thinking about now is what she will wear to the big fancy house.

Mary desperately wants to make an impression. This will be her first trip to the house. She does not want to look like a child on this outing.

She picks out a pair of skinny white jeans, puts on a freshly washed halter top that leaves her flat stomach bare. The cross that Joe gave her last Christmas hangs from her neck.

Think of the money, she thinks.

For Mary, it's incredible money. Several weeks' wages at Mickey D's. And just for giving some old man a massage? She twists the earbuds back in, dives into the closet, sings along with Britney Spears:

Don't you know that you're toxic?

The tight white jeans fit Mary perfectly. She turns to check herself out in the mirror, cropping the scene with her fingers to block out the Barbies behind her. Over on the Gold Coast, girls in big, high-ceilinged bedrooms have American Girl dolls. Dolls with natural smiles, perfectly vacant moon faces. American Girl dolls are beautiful. They're expensive. But you *have* to have one if Mom and Dad are willing to pay. Over on the Coast, most mothers and fathers are. But out in the sticks, where Mary lives, you get Barbies—passed down from mother to daughter, from sister to sister. They're rail-thin, missile-breasted. There's a touch of knowingness to the curl of their otherwise innocent mouths. American Girl dolls are girlie, but Barbie's like Britney Spears. Barbie's dangling her long legs over the line that separates girls from women.

Be like Barbie, Mary thinks.

She *can't* be nervous. Not now. Not today.

What she tells herself, over and over again, is: *It's not that big a deal*.

But, of course, it *is* a big deal. Before long, Mary's visit to the big fancy house will become part of a months-long Palm Beach police investigation—an affidavit for probable cause, filed by the Palm Beach PD—and, finally, the arrest and conviction of the home's owner, Jeffrey Epstein.

CHAPTER 2

Jeffrey Epstein: February 2005

Jeffrey's morning routine is precise and unvarying. First he spends twenty-five minutes in silence, visualizing the day ahead as he digests the guava, banana, and Müeslix that his chef prepares for him—the same way every day—at six in the morning. Then Jeffrey walks a third of a mile up to South County Road, pausing once in a while to take deep, restorative breaths.

It's a slight slope that leads toward the ocean. Jeffrey's home on the Intracoastal Waterway is behind him now. The morning's not windy. The Atlantic is calm and glittery, and fishing trawlers bob gently on distant waves.

Jeffrey's partial to monogrammed sweatpants, monogrammed fleece pullovers, and hoodies. Casual attire offset by embroidered Stubbs & Wootton slippers—the kind that sell for hundreds of dollars a pair. His hair, which is thick, has turned silver. But Jeffrey Epstein does not have a paunch. For a fifty-two-year-old man, he's extremely fit. Six feet tall, 180 pounds, brown eyes, a strong jawline.

He's never been a drinker. He doesn't smoke or take

drugs, and he takes care good care of his body as well as his mind.

It's a magnificent mind. His gift is for numbers: complex calculations, abstract formulas. Even as a child, Jeffrey could untangle math problems that would stump most smart adults. Numbers just fall into place for him, forming in ranks he can bend, twist, manipulate—and *multiply*. He could have been a scientist or a mathematician. As a young man, he taught calculus and physics. Then he became an investor—a very rich man. Then he became a philanthropist, like Bill Gates. His love for science has inspired him to give millions to academics and institutions committed to studying mysteries of the brain and the arcana of physics. He's given millions to Harvard. And he's given money to politicians: Governor Eliot Spitzer, of New York, and Governor Bill Richardson, of New Mexico, where Epstein owns the largest home in the state.

Epstein's flown Bill Clinton to Africa on a private jet—not the Gulfstream he owns but his Boeing 727, customized with its own trading floor—so that the former president could promote his various and worthy causes.

Just for fun, Chris Tucker, the comedian, and Clinton's pal Kevin Spacey had tagged along for the ride.

"Jeffrey is both a highly successful financier and a committed philanthropist with a keen sense of global markets and an in-depth knowledge of twenty-first-century science," Clinton would say through a spokesperson. "I especially appreciated his insights and generosity during the recent trip to Africa to work on democratization, empowering the poor, citizen service, and combating HIV/AIDS."

But is Jeffrey thinking about that trip now?

His first guest is due that morning at nine, and that

leaves him enough time for a shower, a lunch, and a few phone calls before the second girl arrives.

Sarah has scheduled that girl for one.

For Jeffrey, it's just part of the daily routine.

But on *this* day, there's a delicious twist.

One of the girls is a first-timer.

CHAPTER 3

Mary: February 2005

Downstairs, the doorbell is ringing. Mary's father shouts, gruffly:
"Ella está aquí. Su amiga con el camión."
"She's here. Your friend with the truck."

Mary runs down the stairs. It's game day, and Dad's already got the TV on. Her stepmom's out running errands. Mary's twin sister has gone out, too, Rollerblading with a few of her friends.

"Going shopping," she yells, and she pops a piece of Dubble Bubble into her mouth.

"¿Dice quién?"
"Says who?"

Mary's already halfway out the door. Her father calls out again, but on Sundays there's no getting him out of his chair. Besides, Mary knows he'll be happy when he sees the money she's made. *Real* money, like Joe's cousin Wendy Dobbs, is making.* And it's not like she's running

---

* Wendy Dobbs's name, some identifying details, and dialogue have been changed.

off to do something crazy. After all, Wendy's assured her already that there's nothing to worry about.

Mary's father is Cuban—an immigrant—a self-made man who runs a contracting business. He's wise to the ways of the world and highly protective of his two daughters. They're good girls, he knows. Almost angels. As far as he knows, they don't drink. They've never tried drugs. They love clothes and, especially, music—Britney Spears, Nelly Furtado, Maroon 5, the boy band with that dreamy lead singer. Mary loves California, which she's never seen but daydreams about. She just *knows* she'll live there someday—a plan that's okay with her father as long as Mary keeps up with her homework and chores.

What he worries about, in the meantime, is the crowd that Mary runs with.

Joe is a fine boy. More responsible than most American boys his age. But Joe's cousin, Wendy, is another story. Mary's father doesn't like Wendy at all and would have liked her even less had he known about Wendy's intentions.

In just one hour, Wendy's told Mary, she can make more money than her father makes in a day: "This guy in Palm Beach. He's rich. Very rich. He has an airplane. He owns an *island*, you know?"

Like a lot of kids who live inland, away from the Florida coast, Mary's dreams reach way beyond the dull, scrubby flatlands and strip malls she's grown up around. There's so much that she wants to do and see. But for her the Gold Coast, twenty miles away, might as well be another country.

"*Yes*," she had said, without even thinking about it.

Then there was Joe to contend with.

"Who *is* this guy?" Joe had said, shaking his head. "You don't know a thing about him."

"*Hundreds* of dollars," Mary had whispered. She couldn't quite look at Joe, but she was firm: "I can make that in one *hour*."

Joe seemed to think they were actually talking about it. A conversation—some back-and-forth. But the thought of not going hadn't even crossed Mary's mind. If anything, she hoped that it would become a regular thing.

"To rub his *feet*? Are you kidding? If you're not worried about it, why haven't you told your dad?"

"It's your cousin, Joe! Some girls go three times a week."

"The guy's feet must be killing him."

"Shut up!"

"Tell your father."

"You know how Dad is. You don't tell *your* parents everything."

"I'm not going to some freak's mansion to rub his feet."

"That's right. *I* am."

"And if I told your father? Or mine?"

"You'd never see me again."

Mary felt bad as she said it. She felt bad for lying.

She knew that it would be more than a foot rub.

Wendy had told her that much, at least.

CHAPTER 4

Jeffrey Epstein: February 2005

John Kluge, the media magnate, has bought up several lots around here, torn down the mansions, and built a grand, sprawling estate. But Epstein's neighbors have blocked his own efforts to buy more land and increase his holdings.

Epstein's address in Palm Beach is 358 El Brillo Way. Built in the fifties by a totally run-of-the-mill architect, the house has none of the elegance of his neighbors' homes. It's big, with a big swimming pool—that's the most you can say for it. It's totally bland. But it's the last house on a dead-end block, the last block of the street, and this makes it very *secluded*.

Tonight, one of Epstein's black Escalades will whisk him away, taking him to the private terminal at Palm Beach International Airport. Then a short flight down to Little Saint James—or, as he likes to call it, Little Saint Jeff's—the seventy-eight-acre island he owns in the Virgin Islands. But for the moment, there are still things to attend to in Florida. Business *and* pleasure—although, in Epstein's experience, the two have always fit together nicely.

He strolls through the gate, past the guard, up to the side door that leads to the kitchen. Inside, he ignores the maid doing dishes and climbs a wide, winding staircase to the second floor. He walks down a hallway, one that's lined with photographs of naked women. Then, in his bedroom, he opens a closet. Inside, there are many more photographs. Erotic photos, tacked to the wall, of girls who have come to the house.

Familiar faces, familiar bodies. That's what makes the first-timers so special.

Epstein checks his watch before closing the door.

The Virgin Islands can wait.

CHAPTER 5

Mary: February 2005

The Dubble Bubble's lost all its flavor, but Mary's still chewing the gum as she shifts, nervously, in the backseat of Wendy's big pickup truck. The girl sitting up front next to Wendy is a stranger to Mary. She's chain-smoking menthols. The music is blaring; the seat is filthy and gross. Worried that her white jeans will get grody, Mary sits on her hands. Then, through the window, she sees a gigantic resort called the Breakers. It is resplendent, sun-drenched, not quite *real*—like something you'd see in the movies.

It makes for an interesting contrast.

"We'll wait for her," Wendy says to the girl in the passenger seat. "Then we can all go to the mall."

"Which one?"

"The Gardens."

It's like she's not there. Mary wants to say something about it, but she doesn't know if the other girls would even respond. Wendy's always seemed so much cooler than kids Mary's age. This other girl's just a mystery. And when Wendy does turn around to speak to Mary, her stare seems to slice right through the younger girl.

"Remember," Wendy says, according to a probable cause affidavit filed by the Palm Beach police. "When he asks how old you are, say eighteen."

The light changes, and Wendy turns back around but keeps looking at Mary in the rearview mirror.

"Got it?"

Mary nods.

"I mean it," says Wendy.

Who would believe her? Anyone can see that Mary is younger than that.

"*Okay*," she says. "I got it. Eighteen."

Mary takes out her flip phone and sends Joe a text: "Your cousin is a BAMF."

A badass motherfucker.

There's no reply.

"Or maybe she's just a bitch," Mary texts.

Still no reply.

Joe must still be in church, Mary thinks.

They pass El Bravo Way and turn onto El Brillo Way.

Wendy's driving slowly now, right at the speed limit. Once more, she says: "When the man asks your age, say eighteen."

Mary nods again and smiles, slightly. She wants Wendy to see her smiling. To know that she's got it all under control. But Wendy's eyes are on the front gate now. It opens, she parks, and they walk past a guard.

"We're here to see Jeff," says Wendy.

The guard nods—*of course you are*—and leads them to the side door.

They're in the kitchen now. Mary, Wendy, some middle-aged man. The man has a long face, bushy eyebrows, and thick silver hair—and he's *fit*. As fit as the jocks that Mary goes to school with. Not attractive, exactly. He's way too old for that. But confident, in a way that makes an impression.

Standing behind the man there's a woman. She's blond, very pretty, much taller than Wendy.

What a strange scene, Mary thinks. She can't shake the feeling that the man is *studying* her. Then he nods, and he and Wendy walk out of the kitchen. A little while later, they're back.

"Sarah," the man says to the tall woman. "You can take Mary upstairs."

Sarah takes Mary up a wide winding staircase carpeted in pink. Together they walk down a hall that's got photographs on the wall—naked women. Long curtains cover windows and don't let in much light. In the air, there's a strong lavender fragrance.

Then they come to a room containing a green-and-pink sofa. There's a large bathroom off to one side and doors on either side of the sofa. There's a wooden armoire with sex toys on it. There's a massage table, too, and a mural of a naked woman.

"Wait here," says Sarah. "Jeff will be up in a moment."

Mary's too freaked out to do anything else. Fidgeting with her belt loops, she sits on the sofa, jumps up again.

Then she sees *the picture*.

All the girls in the photos are young. But the girl in this one's just a baby.

Much younger than Mary herself.

The girl's smiling, but the smile's mixed with something else—some sort of *anxiety* that's out of place on such a small face. And what she's doing is shocking: pulling her underwear off to the side. Flashing one of her tiny apple-round butt cheeks toward the camera.

Mary gasps. She turns around. And there's Epstein standing in front of her, wearing nothing but a towel.

CHAPTER 6

Michael Reiter: March 2005

Chief Reiter looks more like a bank president than a cop. He's well built, with an air of formality and discretion. But he's got twenty-four years on the job. Decades earlier, he was a campus police officer in Pittsburgh. Then he rose, steadily, through the ranks in Palm Beach, moving up from patrol officer to detective, working vice, narcotics, and organized crime, then becoming a sergeant, captain, major, and assistant chief—a job he held for three years—before becoming chief of police. Reiter is what you'd call seasoned, although chief of police in Palm Beach is a job that calls upon his political skills as much as his street smarts.

Then again, from time to time, things do happen.

Once in a blue moon there are murders—though these are so rare that they tend to be remembered for decades.

Sometimes there are hurricanes to contend with, and, when the sea calms, human cargo washes up on the shore. Sometimes traffickers aim the bows of their boats at the glow of the Breakers resort, order their passengers to go overboard, then tell them to swim.

Most of the passengers are Haitian—men, women, and children who stake all they have on a chance at a life in America. From time to time, Palm Beach cops have to retrieve their bodies from the surf.

Things get busier during the wintertime, or, as the locals call it, the season. It's when the very rich come to town, throw parties and balls, shop, and tangle traffic at the intersections around Worth Avenue. The population booms, and the men and women who work under Chief Reiter deal with fender benders, shoplifters, and snotty skateboarding teenagers. There are DUIs. Domestic disturbances. Choking victims and heart attacks. It's routine stuff, but there's always lots of it. Enough to keep the men and women who work for Reiter busy.

Chief Reiter's proud of the team he has built. And, the team knows, they're lucky to have him. Reiter's extremely well qualified for the job. If anything, he's overqualified, with a certificate from the John F. Kennedy School of Government at Harvard and antiterrorist training at Quantico, courtesy of the FBI. It's not brought up often at cocktail parties in Palm Beach, but several of the 9/11 hijackers lived in Palm Beach County. They took flight lessons at local airstrips. A few, including the mastermind, Mohamed Atta, had been regulars at 251 Sunrise, a chic nightclub in Palm Beach. There they had regaled any woman who would listen with made-up stories about their adventures as pilots.

But 251 Sunrise is shuttered now. The joint was shut down in 2004, after an avalanche of noise complaints. For the moment, Palm Beach is as quiet and calm as any place Reiter has dreamed about.

For the moment.

CHAPTER 7

Mary: March 2005

If there's no traffic, Mary's hometown is less than thirty minutes away from the island of Palm Beach. But in economic terms it's a world away. Her high school is run by the county. Most of Mary's classmates are black. Thirty percent are Hispanic, as she is. The rest are white. The school has a C rating, and lots of students receive free or discounted lunches. Mary is one of those students. But inch by inch, she's working her way out of the crab barrel. A good kid, her teachers think. A kid with a future in front of her.

Weeks have gone by since her meeting with Epstein. She hasn't told anyone about the visit. Still, other kids at the high school have noticed a change.

"Yo, Mary," a friend says. "What's up with you anyway?"

This is a kid who veers from nice to mean, depending on who else is around.

Still, a friend.

"Nothing," says Mary.

"You got your period?"

"Shut the fuck up," Mary whispers.

There have been rumors going around, she knows that. Rumors started by a girl who has eyes for Joe.

"Whore," her rival shouts in the hallway one day.

"You're the whore," Mary shouts back.

Mary rushes the girl, who shoves back, grabbing at Mary's hair, twisting and tugging. Someone yells, "Catfight!" By the time the bell rings for next period, Mary's sitting in the principal's office.

She shakes her head in reply to the questions, stays silent, feeling humiliated.

Then, in her wallet, they find the three hundred dollars.

Mary's too young and too small to be stripping. Besides, the bills are all twenties, not singles or fives. When they call Mary's parents, her teachers suggest a more obvious explanation: Does Mary do drugs or deal them?

Mary's father knows better than that. "No," he insists. A psychologist is called in. And then, Mary does start talking.

Once she does, she can't stop.

It's a wild story. Highly disturbing. A mansion in Palm Beach. A powerful man. This is all far from the principal's wheelhouse. It's *definitely* a matter for the police. In the meantime, the school's recommending a transfer, purely temporarily, to a facility for troubled kids—ones with "issues."

Mary's a good girl, it's true. But further confrontations at the high school will not be tolerated.

CHAPTER 8

Michele Pagan: March 2005

On March 15, Palm Beach police officer Michele Pagan takes the first call from Mary's stepmother.

"Ma'am," she says, "I'm going to have to ask you to come down to the station."

"I don't want to say anything more until I speak with my husband."

"Ma'am, I appreciate that. But I'd urge you to come in. Let us find out what happened. Please."

"I'll get back to you."

"Please, ma'am. I'm here for the rest of the day. We're on South County Road."

At the station, Mary's father does most of the talking.

"There was an incident," he says. "At school. A fight between Mary and another girl. But please understand, our Mary's not like that."

Officer Pagan's starting to feel as though she's swimming in uncharted waters. She's young, and the cases she's worked before this have been minor. Robberies, that sort of thing. Pagan's not used to the Gold Coast. She was educated in New York City, and, to her, the less affluent towns further in from the Coast might as well be somewhere in Georgia. Then again, she knows enough to know that in the back of the station, detectives are already whispering.

What's a guy with that kind of money need with some girl from out west? The women around here could make a man cry.

Extortion?

The kid's fourteen. What would she know from extortion?

Have you seen the shows these kids watch? They know about things we've never dreamed about.

No, Pagan thinks. This is her case.

She's the one who's going to work it.

CHAPTER 9

Mary: March 2005

Mary's father and stepmother believe their girl. Officer Pagan believes Mary's parents. Ergo, Mary must be telling the truth. The girl's got a sweet, high, halting voice. Pagan interviews her twice, and both times, she speaks with her chin buried deep in her chest.

"Tell me, honey," says Pagan. "What happened?"

In her notepad, Michele Pagan writes: *While speaking to me, Mary became upset and started to cry.*

"This white-haired guy came into the room," Mary says. "Wearing only a towel around his waist. He took off the towel. And then he was all naked, and he lay down on a massage table.

"He was a really built guy. But his wee-wee was very tiny."

Mary tells Pagan that Epstein spoke only to give her instructions, which he did in a stern voice. She tells Pagan that she was alone and didn't know what to do.

She removed her pants, leaving her thong panties on, Pagan writes in her incident report.

She straddled his back, whereby her exposed buttocks were touching Epstein's exposed buttocks.

Epstein then turned to his side and started to rub his penis in an up-and-down motion. Epstein pulled out a purple vibrator and began to massage Mary's vaginal area.

Mary's sure that Epstein ejaculated. "He used a towel to wipe himself down as he got off the table," she says.

That week, Pagan's assigned to the case, along with six detectives. Five men, two women. "A predator case," one of them will say. "This is different from someone who is stealing. This predator is a smart person, and that's his *desire*. He can't stop."

Within days, another victim comes into the station. She's got a similar story.

It's a tricky case, according to a source closely involved with the investigation, because the girls involved are far too young to use as bait in an attempt to catch Epstein committing another crime—even if they were willing to play along. Still, there are other strings that Chief Reiter's team can start pulling.

Two weeks later, on March 31, Officer Pagan has Mary make a controlled call to Wendy Dobbs.

The first attempt goes straight to voice mail.

The next time Mary calls, Wendy picks up.

On the recordings made by Officer Pagan, Mary's voice is tiny and tentative, while Wendy sounds mature, gruff, fully grown, like the femme fatale in some old black-and-white movie.

"Hey, what's up?" she says impatiently.

"Nothing," says Mary.

"I talked to Jeffrey, and I'm going to his house tomorrow morning," says Wendy. "I'm going to set something up for you."

"Cool. Like, what do you think?"

"I don't know. I'm going to talk to him tomorrow morning when I go to his house about it."

"Um, how much would I get paid?"

"Talk to him. I'll talk to him tomorrow, and then I'll bring you in the next day. You can talk to him about it."

So far, so good, thinks Officer Pagan. But she needs more. She looks at Mary expectantly, but not too expectantly, she hopes. She can imagine how hard it must be for the girl. Or maybe she can't imagine it at all. But either way, Mary seems to have gotten the message. Straightening up in her chair, she begins to press Wendy.

"I don't know," Wendy says in response. "I don't know. You're going to have to talk to him about it. I mean, I don't really work for him like *that*. I just bring girls to him and they work for him.... You can ask him, like, 'What can *I* do to make more money?'"

Mary keeps pressing.

"The more you do, the more you get paid," Wendy says finally.

"Want me to bring my sister for you? So that we can get paid more or something?"

"Well, yeah. That's what I'm saying. I'm working tomorrow, and me and him are going to put a schedule together for you and your sister. So I'll call you tomorrow when I leave Jeffrey with a schedule."

"Okay, well, I don't have a phone. So if you guys call me, I'd have to know what time so I could get the phone."

"Okay. I'll leave you a message. That's fine. I'll leave you a message."

CHAPTER 10

Noel St. Pierre: March 2005

Noel St. Pierre* thinks of the kids he grew up with in Haiti. His old neighborhood was pressed up against the jungle border that Haiti shares with the Dominican Republic, and some of the kids he knew would slip over. Those kids would stay in the DR for a few days, sometimes weeks. Some of them never returned. But the ones who did come back wouldn't say too much about it.

Most of them didn't talk much at all.

By the time he was ten, Noel had learned the truth about those kids. He'd learned that they'd ended up working as *prostitutes*.

This was how Noel St. Pierre had learned about evil. There really were devils out in the world. Flesh-and-blood devils, and they were nothing like the demons he'd heard about in church. Noel had never forgotten the way those kids looked. The way they'd turned into old men and old women. They were like zombies trapped

---

* Noel St. Pierre is a composite character.

in children's bodies. And now, in America, Noel's been given a chance to help other kids.

That's what the police have told him, at least.

Noel is a sanitation worker. Still strong at fifty, and lucky enough to have found his way to Palm Beach, he gets in to work before anyone else and keeps his white compactor truck clean, almost glistening. His pickup route runs hot and cold with the seasons. But even in the summer, with much less to do, he's on the job early, braced for a six-hour shift that would break a lesser man's back. In the winter, the job gets even harder. The Estate Section gets especially busy. Some of the parties have hundreds of guests. They leave behind mountains of refuse. That garbage gets picked up daily, or twice a day when requested. It's carried by workers who slip, silently, under the porte cocheres. Then it gets whisked twenty miles away to a landfill that the garbagemen call Mount Trashmore.

Noel's stretch of the Estate Section runs from the Everglades Club to the southernmost tip of the island. It encompasses Banyan Road, Jungle Road, El Bravo Way, and El Brillo Way. His performance record is spotless. As far as the Palm Beach PD is concerned, he's the perfect man for the job.

Chief Reiter's authorized a "trash pull"—a legal way to collect discarded evidence. In this case, evidence culled from Jeffrey Epstein's garbage. But when the police call him, Noel St. Pierre simply assumes that another refugee boat has run aground on the beach. A sad thing, but something that does happen from time to time. His homeland, Haiti, is desperately poor. Run by despots who line their pockets while everyday people suffer.

Many of the refugees are illiterate.

Most of them speak only Creole.

"*Eske ou ka ede nou, souple,*" they ask.

"Can you help us, please?"

The cops always need a translator, and Noel's been asked to help out before. But this time the police officer's voice is raspy, impatient.

"This time is different," the officer says. "Something very special. You don't have to accept. But if you do, you'll have to keep things to yourself, completely."

When he hears what the story is, Noel accepts.

"I'll do it," he says immediately.

The address he's been given is 358 El Brillo Way. On his first morning, St. Pierre moves swiftly, sneaking a glance through the kitchen window at the four silhouettes standing inside. Three women, one of them quite short, with pigtails.

The fourth silhouette is that of a tall man.

The police have given him clear instructions. The work is unsavory, but so is the work Noel does every day. What the detectives want from him now are slips of paper with phone numbers, along with toothbrushes, condoms, discarded underwear. Anything that could provide DNA. He's been told to use a special truck on the El Brillo run. Whatever he finds he's to put aside in small trash bags he'll deliver directly to the station at the end of every shift.

Jeffrey Epstein's garbage will never arrive at Mount Trashmore.

As he drives to the police station, St. Pierre thinks about Epstein and what he's been told. It's a wonder to him that American kids would do what the police say these kids have done. American kids are rich, after all. *Some of them just don't know it*, he guesses.

Americans always want more than they have.

Then again, children do stupid things. They don't know any better. And St. Pierre's trips to the house make one thing clear. These girls are young. *Really* young.

"I hope you can stop this man," St. Pierre tells the cop.

The detective shoots him a sharp look, and St. Pierre nods.

"Please," he says, more softly this time.

"Can we count on seeing you here tomorrow?"

The detective looks antsy, impatient again. In his hand he's holding a scrap of paper that Noel St. Pierre has pulled from Epstein's trash. Wendy Dobbs's name is on it. Mary's name is on it as well.

The detective can't wait to get it to Chief Reiter's office.

"As long as it takes, sir," St. Pierre tells him. "Tomorrow, the next day. Whenever you need me."

CHAPTER 11

Michael Reiter: September 2005

There's a sense in which the Palm Beach PD functions as a foundation. From time to time, one of the town's wealthy residents will walk in with a check followed by an inquiry. How much more would the police force need to make this remarkably safe community feel even safer?

A tax write-off? Sure. But why not? Coming from most, it's a genuine gesture. One of appreciation for all they have and for all the department's efforts to guard it. Donations are accepted graciously, gratefully. In 2004, the department had taken one from Jeffrey Epstein—the second donation he'd made to the Palm Beach PD—for ninety thousand dollars. Generous, even by the generous standards of Palm Beach. The donation, which Epstein delivered personally, was earmarked for a firearms training simulator. But that day Michael Reiter had thought something seemed *off* about Epstein.

Something an old cop would notice.

Reiter's officers had told him about complaints they'd gotten a few months earlier—young women hanging around at the end of the block or coming and going at all hours from Epstein's house. "There was some follow-up to that," Reiter said in a deposition for *B.B. vs. Epstein,* a civil suit, brought by a victim, that Jeffrey eventually settled. "I think we may have encountered one or two of them. [We] may have done a little bit of surveillance or talked to neighbors as to whether or not they had seen that. I think we were of the general understanding that, yes, there were very attractive young women coming and going from Mr. Epstein's residence.

"We did some level of further inquiry, and we were of the belief that they were all adults. And [we] were also of the belief that there was a possibility that there could be prostitution. But I mean that's just not something that we heavily pursued—prostitution in private residences; it's common everywhere in America. We didn't believe that they were underage at that point, and so we had no further interest in it."

Reiter had recalled those complaints on the day Epstein had shown up with his $90,000 donation. And when Reiter had walked Epstein downstairs, he couldn't help but notice the tall, beautiful woman whom Epstein had brought with him to the station.

It struck him as strange that she was standing so stiffly, eyes cast downward, as though she were afraid to speak. Not a kid. But not a woman, either. Epstein did not introduce or even acknowledge her. To Reiter, this, too, seemed odd.

Indeed, the statuesque woman was Nadia Marcinkova, a nineteen-year-old beauty who lived at Epstein's home and was described, by another girl, in a recorded interview with Detective Recarey, as one of Epstein's "like, slaves."

In September, several months into the investigation, Epstein calls Reiter directly and asks: Has Palm Beach bought the firearms simulator yet?

Cautiously, Reiter tells him that they're still doing research.

If the department needs more funds, Epstein says, he'll be happy to provide them.

Reiter thanks him graciously and hangs up. But he's certain now that Epstein knows about the investigation. Thinking about Epstein's crimes in Palm Beach makes him shudder. And, Reiter knows, if the charges are true, things are going to get ugly and public.

Cops like Reiter are family men, fathers. Some see so much that they're no longer surprised by the ways of the world. Still, it helps to hold on to a natural capacity for outrage. Thefts are easy to understand: you see something you need, so you take it. Even murders make a kind of sense once you understand the motivation. There's great satisfaction in catching a murderer. But what Epstein's been up to is hard to explain.

Who is this guy?

Reiter's detectives will have to get into Epstein's head. To nail him, they'll have to know him. And to do that, they'll have to get to know the people around him. The police already know about Wendy. That's one procurer, but out of how many?

What kind of person would bring children to a child molester?

And—Reiter can't shake the idea—other victims had to be out there. That lined up with what Epstein's neighbor reported: there were *many* girls. He needed to find them as quickly as possible. It was a race against time.

As long as Epstein was free in Palm Beach, more girls were sure to arrive at the side of the house on El Brillo Way.

CHAPTER 12

Alison: September 11, 2005

It might start with the *Palm Beach Daily News,* which usually covers charity balls, equestrian events, and gallery openings. Reporters there would kill to sink their teeth into something so juicy. On top of that, Chief Reiter knows, Palm Beach is full of freelance paparazzi and seasoned semiretired journalists.

They'd kill for the story, too. For them, it'd be a real-life *Body Heat*.

Over at WPTV, the local NBC affiliate, the phone rings one day.

It's a tip from a kid, sounding nervous. Something about girls from a local high school.

There's a prostitution ring out in Palm Beach, says the boy.

The tip gets brought up in a midmorning meeting at which the producers divvy up ideas among the various reporters and newscasts.

"Where, exactly?" a producer asks.

"He didn't say, exactly," an intern replies. "He said that a very rich man was involved."

"Who?"

"Didn't say."

"Did he leave a call-back number?"

"No. The kid sounded really young. Fourteen, fifteen years old."

The producer thinks for a moment, makes a few scratches in his dog-eared notepad.

"Okay," he says. "I'm not sure what we can do with that for the moment."

At some point, some enterprising journalist will put enough pieces together to get a sense of the picture. Sooner or later, someone will talk. Maybe a parent. Maybe a cop's girlfriend gets giddy at lunch. The girlfriend's girlfriend mentions it to her husband, who says something to a golfing buddy in turn. Maybe the golfing buddy knows a reporter.

Or maybe some lawyer goes *off the rez,* blitzed off those martinis they serve at the Palm Beach Grill.

Sooner or later, there's always talk. At that point, Chief Reiter's job will get much, much harder—with Epstein on one side, the press on the other, and the chief taking flak from all sides. But right now, two months into Reiter's investigation, the press is still speaking in whispers.

Right now, Reiter wants to keep it that way.

And, in the meantime, new pieces of the puzzle keep falling into place.

On September 11, a young woman named Alison gets pulled over by the police.* She's carrying a small amount of marijuana. The patrol officer handcuffs her and puts

---

* Alison's name, some identifying details, and dialogue have been changed.

her in the back of his vehicle. But Alison's been in the back of a police car before, and she's cocky and canny enough to pivot the conversation away from the dime bag she's been busted with. She tells the officer a remarkable story about an older man engaging in sexual activities with high school girls. Alison knows about it firsthand, she says. She's been going to the house on El Brillo Way since she was sixteen.

At first the cop's skeptical. He hasn't heard about the investigation into Jeffrey Epstein's affairs. And, after all, Alison is a burnout. But back at the station, he finds out that Alison has not been bullshitting him.

The investigation is real.

Alison's name and cell phone number match up with messages that have been pulled from Epstein's trash. Instead of copping to a misdemeanor, she becomes another Jane Doe in the case that Chief Reiter's colleague, Detective Joe Recarey, is building against Jeffrey Epstein.

The story Alison ends up telling is extremely disturbing.

Like Mary, she says, she was recruited in high school. She tells cops that Epstein would call her his "number one girl"—although, she suspects, there were many others.

Recarey takes her statement. In the excerpts that follow (transcribed from a tape recording made by the Palm Beach police), *D* stands for "Detective Recarey," and *V* stands for "victim."

D: Well, ah, start from, like, how you met him, and then I'll—I'll take you through.

V: Okay. Um, we [Alison and a female friend] worked at Hollister together in the Wellington Green mall, and I was mentioning to her how I wanted extra money to go to Maine...I wanted to go camping for the summer, and I couldn't afford a plane ticket. And—she goes, "Oh, well, you can get a plane ticket in two hours." I said, "What are you talking about?" Like, what are you—that didn't make any sense to me, a plane ticket in two hours; what are you talking about? And she goes, "Oh, we can go give this guy a massage, and, um, he'll pay two hundred dollars for, like, forty-five minutes or an hour." And that's all she told me—no details, no nothing.

. . .

She said that he wanted cute girls, so I looked cute, did my best. I didn't—I didn't think that it was what it was. I wasn't naive enough to think that he was gonna pay me two hundred dollars just for nothing—I, I don't know, like, I don't know what was going through my head. I absolutely don't know. And I—the back of my mind was thinking, oh, well, it could be legitimate, but I was also thinking, you know, at the same time, is she fucking crazy? Like, this guy's not gonna pay you money for not doing anything, not letting him cop a feel or nothing. You know? So I didn't know what to think, I was like, "Oh...if he does something that I have a problem with, then I'll leave."

. . .

D: Who were you introduced to?

V: One of his girlfriends. One of his, like, slaves that he has live with him. And when I say "slaves," like, one of the girls that he bought to, like, have sex with him. Um, I was introduced to one of them probably, like...Sarah. I was introduced to Sarah. Um, that's his assistant, I think. I think they have sex, but I don't know. Um, I was introduced to his assistant Sarah, and she's the one who told me that he would be ready in a second. And from there I met various other girls. I don't really—I didn't pay attention to who they were, though. . . . So . . . we were waiting on the couch in the bathroom, and, um, Jeffrey comes up, and he's like, "Hey, I'm—I'm Jeffrey." He just introduced himself, and he hands—I remember this 'cause I was pissed off that she got paid to bring me. Like, I was pissed off. He hands her a wad of hundred-dollar bills and says, "Thank you," and she says, "I'll wait for you downstairs," and I was like, "All right, I'll see you in a little while." And that's how I was brought to Jeffrey.

. . .

Um. Hold on—I'm remembering. I'm, like, picturing in my head. I wore a skirt. I remember specifically what I wore: I wore a skirt and just a regular T-shirt. And I was massaging his legs, and he asked me to take off my skirt. And I said—I think I said no at first. And he's like, "Come on, you're not showing"—he talked me into it, basically. He's like, "Oh, you're not showing anything," or [he] did something; I don't even know. So I ended up taking off my skirt, and then he goes—well, I think he just started touching, you know, the top of me. So—and then he asked me.

D: When you're saying "the top of you," you mean your breasts?

V: Yeah. And then he asked me to take off my shirt. So I took off my shirt, but I kept my underwear on. And I wouldn't take my underwear off: I told him no. And he still paid me the same amount. And that was that. I went home.

. . .

D: So, in other words, he—

V: Finished with himself and that was it. Yeah, he ejaculated. Specifically.

D: That was the first time you went there?

V: Mm-hmm.

D: And—I know, take a deep breath, I know, I can see it in your eyes already. From then on, you went there multiple times?

V: I had problems with it. [With] what happened the first time. But three hundred dollars for forty minutes— that was a lot for a sixteen-year-old girl making six bucks an hour.

D: So you're saying you're sure you were sixteen now?

V: Um, I don't want to say I'm sure of my age. I was under seventeen, one hundred percent.

   ...

D: Okay. Um, when you—the first time you went, when he masturbated, did you see?

V: [giggles]

D: His member?

V: Oh, I thought you were going to ask me if I saw, like, his come.

D: No.

V: I saw all of the above.

D: You saw him naked, fully naked? Fully naked?

V: Yeah, a hundred percent naked. He had a towel on for some of it, but that doesn't mean anything. Like, he was naked.

D: He took off the towel?

V: I saw everything, yeah.

   ...

I mean, I'm sorry, he is circumcised, my bad. He's circumcised, a hundred and ten percent sure. A matter of fact, he has some sort of birth defect. On his thing. I don't know what it is [giggles]; I've never really looked at it, because I've never done anything where I had to touch it. I've never touched it—out of the whole time I worked for him, I never touched his penis. Like, he—I'm pretty sure he rubbed it against me, but I've never ever been, like, "Okay, I'm letting you do this" or "I'm gonna do this to you." Um, it's really weirdly shaped. I don't know—do you want me to, like, tell you this?

...

I'm just really embarrassed. Um, it's like a teardrop, like a drop of water. It's really fat at the bottom and skinny at the top, where it's attached. And he never gets fully hard, ever. Like, I just could tell by looking at it—like, by looking you can obviously tell if you're hard or not, and I could tell that he wasn't.

...

D: The next time you went, or as you continued to go, did it escalate more?

V: Mm-hmm. I actually—I don't remember how long it took for me to start working for him regularly, from the first time I went there. But I started working every day. Every single day he was in the country I would be there... And, um, I told him that I wouldn't let him put anything inside of me; that was my rule. Nothing inside of me—no fingers, no, no nothing, absolutely nothing inside of me. He increased my pay to three or four hundred dollars as long as he could touch me. Um, I still never—I, I swear I never touched him, the whole entire time I never, ever touched him. Um, but he, he—

D: How many times would you say you went?

V: Hundreds. Hundreds. I was—he used to tell me I was his favorite. He bought me a car. He bought me—

D: This Jeep that you're driving?

V: No. I had a brand-new Dodge Neon. I got a plane—I got a plane ticket to New York; I got spending money whenever I wanted. Like, I was in there deep. I was—he asked my parents to emancipate me so I could live with him. Or he didn't ask my parents, he asked me to ask my parents, I'm sorry. He actually wanted me to come live with him.

D: As, like, a girlfriend?

V: Sex slave, whatever you want to call it. Yeah. Um, but it escalated—he, he just increased my pay, as long as he could touch me. I wouldn't let him put anything inside of me. And then one day he just did, one day he just put his hand, like, his fingers—and, um ...

D: How long, would you say, from the very first time you went?

V: Months. Honestly, I never kept track, like, of, of what happened when. I just can tell you in which order things progressed.

...

It was—it was, like, towards the middle and end of my school year. But I remember that for the last, like, six or eight weeks of high school, I didn't have a car 'cause I gave it back to him. Because he—he asked me to have sex with him and, like, like suck him and stuff [giggles], and I was just like, no. Definitely not. I was like, "I'll let you touch me, but I'm not gonna do that."

...

Yeah, the car was a Dodge Neon 2005. He got it for me before the New Year, because I remember I got it—it was an edition that was a year before they were supposed to come out. So if I got it, I obviously didn't get a 2006, 'cause that's this year. I got a 2005 Neon in 2004. Seven miles on it when I got it. The car was awesome [giggles].

...

I gave it back before I graduated. It got too— it got too sticky for me. He wanted more than I was willing to give. I didn't wanna—I didn't want to, um, suck his dick. I didn't want to have sex with him. I never did that, and I wanted to be able to walk away from this saying that I—saying that I never did that. And I'm glad that I did.

…

But I lied to him when I gave it back. I didn't want to burn my bridges, because he was a spectacular connection to have. Spectacular. Even if I didn't—even when I didn't work for him. Until this day, he is so aw—he is so—I haven't talked to him in, like, a couple months, but if I called him today he would give me as much money as I asked him for. He doesn't know that I hate him the way I do. I kept that connection. I figured he used me, I'd be able to use him. Um, I hate to say that, but I figured if I wanted to use him I could.

D: Okay. Let me bring you back a little bit.

V: Sure.

D: When did things start to escalate as far as things happening when the massages were given?

V: They escalated whenever he wanted. I don't clearly understand the question.

D: Okay. The first time you went, you were naked—

V: Are you asking for a date?

D: Oh, no, no, no—

V: …and the little steps that things progressed?

D: Right.

V: Well, I went and I wouldn't take off my panties at first. And then he got me to get naked. Then he got me to let him rub me. Then he got me to let him stick his fingers in me. Then he got me to let him go down on me. Then, um—that was pretty much the gist of it, except this one time, where he bent me over the table and put himself in me. Without my permission. And I flipped out. I'm sorry, I didn't ask you, but I don't count that as me having sex with him.... 'Cause I just told you that I never had sex with him. I never did. Even though, I don't know what you'd consider that. But he then—I go, "What are you doing?" He goes, "Oh, I just wanted [redacted] to see this."

D: Okay. Let me back you up. When you were completely naked, the same things happened? You went in, you massaged him?

V: Sometimes I didn't even do that. Sometimes he just asked me to take off my clothes and—he'd have to do work, he'd be sitting at his desk or something, and I'd just be naked there, watching television or reading a book, but I'd be naked. Or, um, sometimes he wanted to just watch TV or read, and he'd lay in his bed and ask me to take my clothes off and lay with him. And that's it. Not touch him or anything.... Sometimes he'd just invite me over for breakfast, for dinner, or just to use the swimming pool, and I'd get paid for that, too. I'd get paid just to hang out with him. That's it. And if the money wasn't there, I wouldn't have ever been in that house.

D: Okay. When he started to touch you—

V: I have a question. Before I say anything else. Um, is there a possibility that I'm gonna have to go to court or anything? Like, that's a possibility, right?

D: Well, here's the thing: When this is all said and done, we're going to sit down, we're going to discuss this. I mean, what he did to you is a crime. I'm not gonna lie to you.

V: Would you consider it rape? Like, would you consider that to be rape, what he did?

D: If he put himself inside you, without permission—

V: I didn't say that, or anything. I was standing up and the table is about, like, my hip length—he just put me down—

D: That, that is a crime. That is a crime.

V: I don't want my family to find out about this. My family doesn't know any of this. My mom thinks I was his secretary, for two years, or however long—a year and a half. My mom thinks I made phone calls for him and that's how I was making my [unintelligible] money. That's it. I don't want her to know anything.

D: Well, you're an adult. You're an adult now.... When we're done with this interview, we'll discuss this further and we'll decide the best course.

V: 'Cause Jeffrey's gonna get me. You guys realize that, right? He's gonna find—he's gonna figure this out. And he's gonna—I'm not safe now. You understand that, right? I'm not safe.

D: He is not this person that he is portraying himself to be—

V: Well—

D: Why do you say you're not safe? Has he said he's hurt people before?

V: Well, I've heard him make threats to people on the telephone, yeah. Of course.

D: You're gonna die? You're gonna break your legs? Or—

V: All the above! But that's not the point.

D: Who's he talking to?

V: I don't know. I don't know, I heard those conversations, I mean, I've been in the room when he was on the phone and [unintelligible] threatened. Like, I witnessed lots of things. I just don't know what, specifically, you all [want to know].

D: Everything.

V: I used to go there every day, like I w—I don't, I don't know how many other girls he was saying, "You're my favorite, and I want you to live with me" to, but I was in about as deep as you can get.

D: He had quite a few girls he would say that to.

...

D: Do you have any formal massage training?

V: [Giggles.] Hell, no.

D: All right, I was just asking.

...

V: He would kiss me and stuff, too. I remember that. And when he kissed me, if he was jerking off he would, like, rub himself on my breasts. And I...I was extremely uncomfortable. I would maneuver myself away from that activity. I'd get up and I'd move somewhere else, or I'd—I don't even remember. I would stop whatever was going on without saying, "Can you get the fuck off me?" I would stop it without saying stuff like that.

D: Okay.

...

V: I wouldn't let him put anything in me until one day he did just out of nowhere. And I said, "Wait a second: my boyfriend, you know, we had this thing, you can't do that. You know, I'm—I'm allowed to work here as long as you don't do that." And he said "okay." Well, a couple months later I guess he assumed me and my boyfriend had broken up, and he just did it one day; he just did it without asking or anything. And then I said, "What are you doing?" I said, "You know that's not cool," and he goes, "Oh, I thought we did that last time." And I said, "No, we did not do that last time." And then he goes— uh, and then he just offered me more money. He's like, "Well, why don't I just give you something extra, and we can try this out?" And I was like [sigh], "All right." Very hard guy to say no to. I don't know if any of you guys ever talked to him....

...

Oh, yeah. Well, if you talk to him, I mean, he straight up tries to control the situation. Every—every word that comes out of your mouth, it seems like, he knows what you are going to say. Like, that's his job; that's how he made his money is knowing what people are gonna say and what people are gonna do.

D: What did he tell you he does for a living?

V: Well, there's a couple of things. Things that I found for myself, things I looked up on the Internet. What he specifically told me when I asked him the first time was, "Oh, I'm a brain scientist." And I said, "What the fuck is a brain scientist?" I was like, "That's not a real job—tell me the truth." But anyway...his explanation was, "It's my job to know how people's brains work." And I said, "Whatever the fuck that means. Whatever. You're like some old guy who [unintelligible....]" You know what he promised me? Here's the reason I held on so long is, he promised me that I would get into NYU. That I would get into NYU and he would pay for it. And I waited, and I waited, and I scored great on my SATs, I would get 4.0—like, I did great in school. I filled out my application and he told me that it wasn't good enough. So I filled it out again, and it was like three times. So I'm pretty sure he wasn't checking into it, he was just telling me that he was. But I think that had a lot to do with the reason I stayed there so long, 'cause my dream was right in front of me, you know? And it's so far....

D: Aside from having been with [redacted], was there anybody else that you brought to the house?

V: I brought a few people.... Because it got out that I did this. Like, everyone at school knew. You know, everyone talks—

D: It was a circle, and—

V: It was a little circle, yeah.... Not that I would want anybody to get involved.... I brought girls I didn't like and, frankly, did not give a shit about. Girls that I knew were skanks. That would do anything. Girls that would just, like, suck dick in the bathroom at school. Like, not even people I was friends with. I'd just hear a rumor about a girl and be like, "Hey, I know a way you can make two hundred dollars. How about..." I would tell them flat out, like, "This is what you've got to do. Are you cool with this? 'Cause I'm not gonna take you if you're not." So I told them. They all know that I got paid to bring them. It was actually [redacted]. She took off her shirt. She was a little overweight, so he didn't want anything to do [with her]. She was my best friend. But, you know, she was another story. I did care about her. But, um, she lost her house and stuff and really needed money. She had— she was homeless, she had nowhere to go. So she did it out of desperation.

...

D: Did he ever hurt you?

V: Sometimes he got violent, yeah.

D: Violent as in what? As in—

V: He pulled my hair a lot harder than it should have been pulled. Like, he—okay, I can understand having sex, and you're all, like, not—not that we were having sex, but I mean, like, if you're all into it and you pull hair a little bit, like, my ponytails—just like a little bit, whatever. But he would pull it to where it would rip my hair out. It would rip my hair, and then sometimes he would pick me up and, like, throw me whichever way he wanted me, and then he would just like use a toy or, like, his hand or whatever. Never his penis, though, ever. I never had sex with him. But um—I'm little, so he could pick me up. Like, if you pick me up and throw, obviously it's gonna hurt....

. . .

I mean, there's been nights that I walked out of there barely able to walk, um, from him being so rough. But nothing really—nothing specific that he really got violent with. Like, I can't really recall.

. . .

Nothing that I went to the doctor for, no. I mean, I remember getting tore up a few times, but it was nothing that—

. . .

D: This is getting real personal, but were you active before him?

V: What, like, had I had sex? Yeah [laughs].

D: Okay.

V: Um. But honest, I mean, I'm not—I'm not a ho. I've had only three steady boyfriends, and those are the only three that I've ever done anything with. And they were all with me for over a year. So it's not like I just go and hook up at parties.

. . .

Like, I've gotten thousands of dollars' worth of shit. Man, the underwear I'm wearing right now he gave me. Like, I'd—I'd go over there and there'd be a bag of Victoria's Secret underwear, like, waiting for me, like, talking, like, fifteen hundred dollars' worth of stuff. I got a plane ticket from him once. I got a car,

I got Christmas bonuses, I got movie tickets. Like, he'd buy me movie tickets—like, he'd say, "Hey, have you gone to the movies lately?" I'd be like, "I dunno, oh—not really," [and] he goes, "Do you want to go?" He'd give me, like, eight movie tickets. I got show tickets; I went and saw, like, David Copperfield. I had, like, VIP tickets or something like that.

...

I need to show you, like, what I'm talking about, like, the positioning that we were—it was like, okay, here's the thing: there's the, like, little flower thing, then here's the massage table. I was right here, he was right here, [and] she was here. Um. And I was standing up, and he just pushed me over the table, and he did his thing with me.

D: Okay. Were you facing the table? Were you?

V: I was. I was facedown on the table. Like, facedown, hands, like, on my head, holding—I don't, I don't mean—I wasn't fighting, really. So I don't know if he was holding me down to kinda stop me from fighting or what he was doing. He's just a really weird— he's into really weird stuff. Like, I was just bent over, and my face was on the table. I was facedown on the table. And then he did his thing. So. But anyway, [redacted] was right here, and I'm pretty sure she was naked, and the couch is, like, right behind, but, um, that's how it happened.... He was only in me for, like, a minute or two. I don't even know if you could say that long. He put it in, did a couple of pumps, or whatever the fuck you wanna call it, and I was like, "What are you doing?" [giggles] I go, "What are you doing?" He's like, "Oh, I just wanted [redacted] to see this." Then that was that.

CHAPTER 13

Wendy Dobbs: October 3, 2005

Every chance he gets—and he gets lots of chances—Chief Reiter drills the same thing into his investigators' heads: they need to be careful. Patient. Methodical. Strategic. Or Epstein's lawyers will eat them for lunch.

Inch by inch, they move their case toward the goalpost. But in October, Detective Recarey and his coworkers catch a break that moves the ball several yards down the field.

On the first Monday of that month, they pick Wendy up at her house and, down at the police station, she starts to sing—like a *bird*.

The detectives can hardly believe it or get it all down fast enough. Later on, in a probable-cause affidavit, Detective Recarey will write:

Approximately two years ago, just after she turned 17 years of age, [Wendy] was approached by a friend named Molly at the Canopy Beach Resort in Riviera Beach. [Dobbs] was asked if she wanted to make

money. She was told she would have to provide a mas-
sage and should make $200. [Dobbs] thought about
the offer and agreed to meet with Jeffrey.

Molly (Unknown last name) and Tony (Unknown
last name) picked [Dobbs] up and she was taken to
Epstein's house. Upon her arrival to the house she was
introduced to Epstein in the kitchen of the house. She
was also introduced to a white female known to her
as Sarah. She was led upstairs to the main bedroom
known to her as Jeff Epstein's bedroom.

Sarah arranged the massage table and covered the
table with a sheet. She brought out the massage oils
and laid them next to the massage bed. Sarah then left
the room and informed [Dobbs] Jeff would be in, in
a minute. Jeff entered the bedroom wearing only a
towel.

He removed the towel and laid nude on the mas-
sage table. He laid on the table onto his stomach and
picked a massage oil for [Dobbs] to rub on him.

"He tried to touch me, and I stopped him," says
Dobbs.

I asked how he tried to touch her. [Dobbs] stated that
Epstein grabbed her buttocks and she felt uncomfortable.

"I'll massage you," Dobbs had told Epstein. "But I
don't want to be touched."

[Dobbs] stated she performed the massage naked. At
the conclusion of the massage, Epstein paid [Dobbs]
$200.

After the massage Epstein stated to [Dobbs] that
he understood she was not comfortable, but he would
pay her if she brought over some girls. He told her

*the younger the better. [Dobbs] stated she once tried
to bring a 23-year-old female and Epstein stated that
the female was too old. [Dobbs] stated that in total
she only remembers six girls that she brought to see
Epstein. Each time she was paid $200. [Dobbs] said at
the time she brought these girls to Epstein's house they
were all 14 through 16 [years] of age.*

Wendy Dobbs keeps talking. What she says about
Mary's visit lines up neatly with what Mary's already told
the police. Wendy's own experience with Epstein syncs
up, too. But Wendy's not a victim, as Mary is. After all,
she's been playing on Epstein's team. Team *predator.*

A police sergeant enters the room. What he wants to
know is, does Wendy realize that she's implicated herself
in Epstein's crimes?

Beads of sweat form on Wendy's forehead, and now
the police know they've really got her. She gives them
phone numbers to go with the young girls she's named.
She provides addresses. But no, Wendy doesn't quite get
it. On the way home, in a police car, she brags in the
backseat:

"I'm like a Heidi Fleiss," she tells the escorting officers.

CHAPTER 14

Wendy Dobbs, interview with Detective Recarey and Sergeant Frick, October 3, 2005, transcribed from video (excerpts)

RECAREY: Okay. Your Pepsi's coming, my Pepsi's coming. First of all, I know you're freaking out. Don't freak out, just relax. Okay? I want to thank you for coming. All right? Though the door's closed, you're free to go at any time. You're not here—you know, it's only closed for our privacy.

DOBBS: That's fine.

RECAREY: I understand that you may have information on a case that we're looking into, okay? That's the reason why I brought you here today. All right? And again, you're here voluntarily. You agreed to come back with us and talk to us. But I do want to talk you about Jeff Epstein, and the whole...thing.

DOBBS: And I don't need a lawyer, right?

RECAREY: It's up to you. If you wanted one, you can have one. I can't tell you yes or no on that. That's totally [up] to you, I'm only—

DOBBS: I'm not gonna get in trouble for anything I say, right?

RECAREY: Right now, you're just a witness. I'm talking to you as a witness.... That's totally up to you. You wanna talk to me?

DOBBS: I have no problem telling you everything I know. I'm a very cooperative person.

RECAREY: Okay. How did you first meet, um—

DOBBS: I first met Jeffrey—I was at a beach resort on Singer Island, and I was approached by this girl I went to school with. Her name was [redacted]. And she was asking me, you know, "Oh, you need extra money, I know this guy...." I thought about it and I finally gave her a call, and her and her friend [redacted] met up with me. I actually picked them up and we drove down to Jeffrey's house. She introduced me, whatever.

RECAREY: Okay. Now, what [do] you mean by making money, how do you make money with Jeffrey?

DOBBS: Um, there's two ways. There's two ways you can make money. He'll, all right—

RECAREY: That's all right. Talk to me. Talk to me like, like nothin'.

DOBBS: How do I say—this is going to sound really sleazy, but—

RECAREY: No. Go ahead. Talk to me.

DOBBS: Every girl that meets Jeffrey starts off with giving him a massage. The more you do with him, the more you make. Basically, if you take off your clothes, you're gonna make more. If you let him do things to you, you're gonna make more.

RECAREY: Like "do things" you mean, touch you?

DOBBS: Yeah. Touch you in inappropriate places.

RECAREY: Okay. Does he use his hand? Does he—

DOBBS: He uses his hands and, I really wouldn't call it a vibrator—I guess it's like a massager? But um—I was one of the girls that refused to do that. I did it basically my—I did it naked, but I wouldn't let him touch me or anything like that. So after that he's like, "You know what?" He's like, "Listen, I'll pay you $200 for every girl that you bring to me." He's like, "I don't want you to massage me anymore, you know, just bring girls to me...." So that's the other way you can make money. For every girl that you bring to the table—so, for every girl that I brought to Jeffrey—I would make $200. Flat. Just right there.

RECAREY: Just to bring a girl.

DOBBS: Yeah. Just to bring a girl.

RECAREY: Okay. And the girl that was going knew that she would have to massage him.

DOBBS: She knew everything. She knew everything. That was one of Jeffrey's rules. He had a problem with girls coming to the house that didn't know what they were getting into. He would tell me, you know, "Make sure these girls know what I expect, make sure they know what they want, because when I get in that room I don't want them to—you know—they need to know." And, as far as [redacted]'s case, she knew everything she was getting herself into. It was all volunteer.

RECAREY: Okay. What did you tell her that she was gonna do?

DOBBS: I told her the same thing. I told her, you know, this guy Jeffrey—she came to me saying she needed money, da da da. I basically told her about it. She was like, um, you know, "What do you have to do?" I told her. I was like, "The more you do, the more you make. That's it. In order to make money, you're gonna have to go up there. You're gonna take your clothes off. But the more you do, is the more you make." She walked out of there with $300. So she obviously and evidently let him do a little more. Plus, on our way home, she kinda told me what she did.

RECAREY: Which was? Give the massage....

DOBBS: She gave the massage, and she basically let him, like, touch her, down there. Basically.

RECAREY: Did he touch her with his hands?

DOBBS: All with his hands. And then he brought out the massager. From what she told me.

...

RECAREY: How old were you when you were approached to see Jeffrey?

DOBBS: Um, I think I was seventeen?

RECAREY: Seventeen.

DOBBS: Sixteen or seventeen.

RECAREY: Okay. When was the last time you talked to him?

DOBBS: It's been a while. I can honestly say it's probably been about close to a year. About a year. I actually stopped working for him.

RECAREY: Who was the last girl you brought over?

DOBBS: The last girl I brought over was [redacted]....

RECAREY: Okay. You got paid two hundred bucks for taking her over?

DOBBS: Yes.

RECAREY: Okay. [Redacted] knew ...

DOBBS: She knew everything.

RECAREY: That she'd have to massage him, and the more she did—

DOBBS: The more she'd make.

RECAREY: The more she got paid.

DOBBS: Yeah.

RECAREY: So, she had intercourse with him.

DOBBS: Um, I don't know about the intercourse. I heard different stories on that. I've never asked him "Oh, you know…" But when I was first introduced to him, my friend [redacted] who introduced me to him, told me that she knew a girl who slept with him and made $1,000. But from what his intern—or secretary—told me, is that he doesn't do that. He just plays around with them. So I heard two different stories.

 …

RECAREY: So, when you went and you massaged him, nothing happened between you two.

DOBBS: Nothing. I wouldn't let him.

RECAREY: Okay. Did he become forceful? Did he get upset?

DOBBS: I wouldn't say he became upset. I think he was a little disappointed. But I'm not—I didn't care. I knew I was getting paid. I let him—I let him look, but I never let him touch. It was out of the question for him. And I think that's pretty much why he just, kind of down-promoted me? He was just kind of like, "You can bring girls." But as far as working, you know—

RECAREY: Okay. How many girls have you brought to him, aside from [redacted]?

DOBBS: Oh. Um. A lot.

RECAREY: A lot?

DOBBS: Um, let's see, there's [several redacted names]….

RECAREY: And all these girls knew what they had to do?

DOBBS: Every one of them.

 …

RECAREY: How long have you been working for him?

DOBBS: Um…I probably worked for him for a year.

RECAREY: Okay. And out of all these girls…

DOBBS: Those were all the girls I brought. But you have to remember, those girls brought other girls, too.

RECAREY: Oh, okay.

DOBBS: So it's like—it's like a train. It's like, I introduced him to all my friends, and then...it goes on and on, like that.

...

RECAREY: Okay....[Redacted] being fourteen or fifteen at the time—I think [redacted] was fourteen when this happened—who else was underage? Out of all these?

DOBBS: Underage, what do you mean?

RECAREY: Under eighteen.

DOBBS: Under eighteen? All of 'em.

RECAREY: All of them?

DOBBS: All of them....

RECAREY: Okay. Did Jeff know anybody's real true age? Or he didn't care.

DOBBS: I don't think he cared. He told me the younger the better.

RECAREY: The younger the better. All right.

DOBBS: Pretty much. That's how it worked. He didn't—let me just put it this way: I tried to bring him a woman who was twenty-three, and he didn't really like it.

RECAREY: Didn't go for it.

DOBBS: It's not that he didn't go for it. He just didn't care for it. And he likes the girls that [are] between the ages of, like, eighteen and twenty....But some of them, I think, lie about their age. I know that when I started off young, I think he knew better [than] to believe me. I think he knew that I was younger—like, seventeen—but I told him I was, like, eighteen. Most of those girls lie when they go in there.

...

RECAREY: Let's talk about [Mary] for a minute.

DOBBS: Okay.

RECAREY: [Mary] at the time was dating your cousin, right?

DOBBS: Mm-hmm.

RECAREY: Okay. She told you she needed to make money. Did she know you worked for Jeffrey?

DOBBS: I told her.

RECAREY: You had told her you worked for Jeffrey.

DOBBS: Mm-hmm.

RECAREY: Did you tell her what it entailed? So she knew that?

DOBBS: She knew everything before she even agreed to it.

RECAREY: Okay. So she knew that there was going to have to be some kind of—

DOBBS: Contact. Pretty much. Yeah. I told her. I told her exactly what his expectations were. I told her what goes on with the girls that go up there. I told her—it was like, "It's your call." I was like, "If you want to do this, fine. If not, fine. But when you go in that room, I don't want to hear you say, 'Oh, I didn't know he was going to do all that.' Because I'm telling you right now, he's expecting it."

RECAREY: Basically, this is touching—

DOBBS: Fondling—

RECAREY: Fondling—

DOBBS: Or whatever. And I told her when she went on her own. Just like, "Just remember, the more you do, the more you make. But that's—that's up to you." And she asked me, and I brought up, told her *I* wouldn't do more.

RECAREY: Okay. You made that clear, you wouldn't do more.

DOBBS: No. Screw that!

RECAREY: But as far as [Mary] is concerned. What did she tell you that happened in that room?

DOBBS: Exact words? If I can recall, when she came downstairs from—when she came downstairs, me and her and [redacted], we all walked out. We got into the car. And I was like, "How much did you make?" She's like, "Three hundred dollars." And I looked at [Mary] and I just knew right then she did more.

RECAREY: Than just a massage, right?

DOBBS: Yeah. And I asked her. I was like, "Well, what'd you do?" She's like, "Well, I started giving a massage, and then my clothes came off and, you know, he put his fingers inside me. And then he brought out the massager." And that's basically what she said.

...

RECAREY: It's all right. You can talk to me. It's all right.

DOBBS: It's kind of incredible talking about it, now that I—I can't believe I worked for him.

RECAREY: But it's okay. You know what, we all go through things in life, you know what I mean? It's an experience. And you can put this experience behind you.

...

Do girls that—people that you brought over—how did you approach them? That they were going to have to do this... Like, if they wanted to work, how did you approach them? Say, "Listen, I got this guy in Palm Beach?"

DOBBS: Um... Two of them were my friends. The others were, like, my acquaintances. It was a little more easier talking to them about it, 'cause, like, I knew them.

RECAREY: Take a deep breath. Take a deep breath. 'Cause I can see you're working up again. You're working up the tears, I can see it, and I don't want to get you like that.

DOBBS: I, um, pretty much I just would ask them—

RECAREY: Straight up?

DOBBS: "If you're looking for extra money, let me know; this guy down in Palm Beach, he's really, really, really wealthy. You have to give him a massage." That's all I would tell them. Then, if they were interested or told me, "Yes, I want to do it," I'd go into detail with them before they'd actually agree. If they told me, "Yeah, that sounds good, I'm interested," then I'd tell them, "Okay, well I'm gonna let you know, this is what you have to do, this is what's gonna go on."

RECAREY: Did you tell them that you were going to make money from bringing them over? Or—

DOBBS: Most part? I believe they knew. . . . Most of the girls, we were open about that. We didn't—they pretty much knew I was making money under the table. So . . .

RECAREY: Okay. Gimme two seconds. Let me get the soda. . . . Gimme two seconds.

. . .

All right, I talked to my boss a little bit—

FRICK: —Which is why I'm here.

DOBBS: Okay.

FRICK: Obviously I was listening to what you were saying. And at this point you clearly implicated yourself on a crime, okay? You've taken girls to somebody's house for the purpose of prostitution. More importantly, more significantly, one of those girls was fourteen at the time, okay? Now that's a pretty significant second-degree felony, okay? I'm not going to kid you, that is—it's a significant thing, okay? Now, you came in, you cooperated with us. The question we have for you now is, do you want to continue cooperating with us and try and help us make a case against Jeff?

DOBBS: I don't think that's really going to help me in the long run, though. I've already admitted to a second-degree felony, right?

FRICK: Yeah, you have.

DOBBS: Okay, so there you go. What's going to keep me out of trouble? It's not going to keep me out of trouble. I've already admitted committing a crime.

FRICK: I'm not going to argue with that....

DOBBS: So basically I just fucked myself. I can go two ways. I can agree not to cooperate, which is going to put me at—well—now you can use the second-degree felony against me. Or you can help and work with it and maybe get myself some slack....

FRICK: We're still talkin' here. What would the odds be of you contacting Jeff at this point? Have you had any contact with him at all?

DOBBS: I have not had any contact—

FRICK: How about with—

DOBBS: No, none of 'em. None of 'em.... I had a phone call about four or five months ago, and I told my parents. Look, I swear to you I'm not anywhere—like, no connection with him at all. That's why I pretty much got my number changed. I have not made any communication with him. It stopped.

FRICK: Okay. Well, I mean, that's good. That's good that you stopped....

...

This is what we'd like to do: We would like to reach out to some of your ex-friends and [unintelligible] talk to them. Now, the question is, do we think that they are currently still working for Jeff, in which case they would make a phone call to Jeff? Or can we just kinda show up and, you know, have you make a call as we're standing outside and say: "Hey, you know, these guys wanna talk to you, and I've already told 'em everything?" Our goal is to make a better case against Jeff, all right?

RECAREY: With your cooperation.

FRICK: Let me, let me get back to—past—the cooperation thing, okay? There are lesser charges that can easily be filed: leading to the delinquency of a minor, as compared to a second-degree felony. You know what I mean? That's a misdemeanor.... First of all, I'll tell you straight up, okay, we're not going to take you to jail today....

DOBBS: Not today.

FRICK: Well, you're—And here's the other thing: If you cooperate and if we can—If you cooperate, whether we pull it off or not—that's not up to you, that's up to us, okay? So what we would do is if we ended up charging you with like a misdemeanor, we'd give you a call, we'd say: "Hey, you gotta come in, you know."

RECAREY: You sign it....

FRICK: That's our preference. You come in, you've been very forthright with us, you've been very up front—

RECAREY: Very truthful.

. . .

FRICK: Do you want us to call your parents, or do you want to deal with it, or do you—As far as we're concerned you're an adult, okay? You're nineteen. You do what you do. You know, we can drop you off at the end of the block if you'd like. Or we can cushion the blow beyond what—but again, you're helping us at this point. We've been pretty forthright with you on what is going on, our options for your future. And what we'd like you to do obviously is make a couple of calls with us this evening to talk to a couple of your, you know, these other girls.

DOBBS: I'm not really on a . . . Me and my parents really don't get along right now . . .

FRICK: So you'd prefer that—

DOBBS: If they found out that I was—If they found out that I was into some other stuff. . . . I'm actually stripping now. . . . So they're not exactly happy with me at the moment, and I don't want to do anything that's going to piss 'em off even furthermore.

CHAPTER 15

Michael Reiter: October 3, 2005

Chief Reiter sifts through the evidence: information about underage girls—six of them—whom Wendy Dobbs procured for Epstein. Phone numbers pulled from the trash on El Brillo. An arrest report for Alison, the girl who'd been caught with a dime bag of weed.

She'd told Detective Recarey about an encounter that sounded very much like a rape.

Soon Reiter will ask a judge for a warrant. But not yet. There's more footwork to do, and Reiter calls Detective Joe Recarey into his office.

Later that day, Detective Recarey and Sergeant George Frick arrive at the home of a girl named Jenny.* An older woman greets them at the front door and invites them inside. She introduces them to her husband and daughter. Jenny is sixteen years old. Sitting down at the dining room table, they see that she's nervous. In between biting

---

* Jenny's, Francine's, and Kristina's names, some identifying details, and dialogue have been changed.

her lip and fidgeting, she tells them that yes, she's been to Jeffrey Epstein's house.

Wendy took her there once. But nothing much happened. She met Epstein's chef and spent some time in the kitchen is all. Then she left.

"I get what you're asking," she says. "But really, I just want to put the whole thing behind me."

"Okay," the officers tell her. "You have our numbers. But Jenny, if you remember anything else, you'll find that we're very good listeners."

One down. Five to go.

Detective Recarey and Detective Michael Dawson have better luck the next day with Francine, a girl who tells them that a year earlier, Wendy Dobbs—someone she knew from high school—drove her to the house on El Brillo Way.

Francine would have been seventeen at the time.

Now she's willing to make a sworn statement. The officers noted:

She was told she could make money working for Jeff. She was told she would have to provide a massage for Jeff....She was brought to the kitchen area by [Dobbs]. They met with the house chef who was already in the Kitchen area. Francine stated [Wendy] would wait for her in the kitchen.

Just as she did with Mary, a woman named Sarah had taken Francine upstairs and into a bedroom. Then Epstein had entered the room, wearing only a towel.

She kept her clothes on during the massage. She advised sometime during the massage, Epstein grabbed

*her buttocks and pulled her close to him. Francine said
she was [made] uncomfortable by the incident involving Jeff. At the conclusion of the massage she was paid
$200.00 for the massage.*

"Do you have any formal training in massages?" the
officers ask.

"No," says Francine.

But she does have one more thing to tell them.

Sarah's been calling Francine's cell phone.

It could mean any number of things. The police
know already that Epstein's caught wind of their investigation. Now it appears he's doing something about it,
or at least he's delegating the responsibility. This troubles the cops. But then, on that same day, they get one
more break: Jenny calls and says that without her parents
around she's willing to make a sworn statement.

It turns out that Jenny's visited with Epstein several times.

And, it turns out, she'd done much more than sit in
the kitchen. Without her parents around, she's much
more willing to talk about it.

The first time she'd gone to the house on El Brillo
Way, she says, Epstein had tried to take off her shirt.
She'd become upset, and this had led to a fight—a "ver-
bal disagreement"—with Epstein.

She'd left without getting paid. Gone down to the
kitchen and told Wendy, "Let's go!"

"If you're uncomfortable," Wendy had told her, "tell
him to stop, and he will."

On the other hand, Wendy had also told her, "The
more you do, the more you get paid."

A few weeks later, she agreed to return to the house
on El Brillo.

Once again Sarah had taken Jenny upstairs and into the master bedroom. Sarah had set up the massage table, laid out the oils that Jenny would use.

Then Epstein had entered the room wearing only a towel.

Jenny had been wearing tight jeans. She had a tight belt on. She kept the jeans on, though Epstein still made a grab for her buttocks. Then he rolled onto his back and grabbed for her breasts. Jenny became upset yet again. But this time, she was paid two hundred dollars before leaving. She never did go back to the house. But, like Francine, she has one more thing to tell the detectives.

Another girl from her high school had been there on the day of her second visit with Epstein. Kristina. And later, Kristina told Jenny that she also had "a problem" with Epstein.

Girls seemed to be turning up all the time. And the detectives were just getting started.

One girl leads Chief Reiter's team to another. And every time, they hear the same story. The girls are approached by Wendy Dobbs. They drive over to Epstein's house. After a short wait in the kitchen—maybe some milk and cereal, if they feel hungry—they're walked upstairs. Epstein's there, waiting, wearing his towel. Sometimes with a vibrator. Sometimes the girls recommend their friends, and for this they receive a commission.

None of the girls comes from money. And none of them has been trained as a masseuse. Then again, how could they be? To become a licensed massage *apprentice* in Florida, you need to be eighteen years old, at least, and have a high school diploma or GED.

CHAPTER 16

Cynthia: October 6, 2005

T hree days after meeting with Francine, the police drive to Boca Raton. They're there to see Cynthia Selleck, who's eighteen years old.* But according to the probable-cause affidavit that the Palm Beach PD is preparing in order to obtain an arrest warrant for Epstein, Cynthia was sixteen when Wendy Dobbs first took her to meet him.

During a sworn taped statement, she tells the police that she'd met Wendy at her high school. She says that Wendy had recruited her and prepped her for her first visit to Epstein's house. And she says she'd ended up going to the house "a lot of times to provide massages over the past two years." The affidavit states:

> *She considered Epstein a pervert, and he kept pushing to go further and further until [Cynthia] explained she would keep telling him she had a boyfriend.*

---

* Cynthia Selleck's name, some identifying details, and dialogue have been changed.

Only recently, Cynthia says, did she begin to remove her clothes in the course of giving Epstein massages.

"Jeff would try to get away with more and more on each massage," she tells the cops.

Still, Sarah had Cynthia's cell phone number, and Sarah would call whenever Epstein was in Palm Beach to make an appointment for "work."

> *Each time she went, Sarah would meet her at the kitchen door area. She would bring her upstairs and prepare the massage table. [Cynthia] advised Epstein would ask her questions about herself. Epstein knew she was a soccer player and would be attending [a nearby] university.*

The cops want to know: Did Epstein know her real age?

> *[Cynthia] stated Epstein did and didn't care. The most recent massage she provided was on October 1, 2005.*

October 1.

That's less than a week ago.

What the cops know now is that Epstein's still at it.

What they're about to learn seals Epstein's fate.

CHAPTER 17

Alison: October 11, 2005

After speaking with Cynthia, Detectives Recarey and Dawson meet up, once again, with Alison. It's been exactly one month since her arrest, and once again, she's willing to talk. They have no trouble obtaining her sworn taped statement.

Alison is eighteen, but she's been going to Epstein's house since 2002. Things got off to a slow start, she says. She received two hundred dollars for her first session, during which she had her bra off but her underwear on. Still, at the end of the session, Epstein had asked for her number.

Then the sessions got heavier. *Much* heavier, as Detective Recarey already knew. *[Alison] stated that during her many visits a routine was established between her and Epstein,* he wrote in his report.

She would enter the house and get naked in the bedroom. She would then start with a back massage. Epstein would roll on to his back and allow her to massage his chest area. [Alison] stated Epstein would then begin to masturbate himself and at the same time would insert his fingers in her vagina and masturbate her with his fingers.

[Alison] explained Epstein would continue this process until he ejaculated. He would then utilize a vibrator/massager on her vagina until [Alison] climaxed. [Alison] advised that during her frequent visits, Epstein asked for her real age, [and Alison] stated she was sixteen. Epstein advised her not to tell anyone her real age. [Alison] advised that things escalated within the home as Epstein would instruct and pay [Alison] to have intercourse with his female friend, Nada Marcinkova [sic]. [Alison] explained the intercourse included using strap on dildos, large rubber penis'[sic] and other devices that Epstein had at his disposal. Epstein would watch them have intercourse and masturbate himself. Occasionally, Epstein would then join in during the female on female intercourse and provide oral sex to both [Alison] and Marcinkova. This occurred during the time [Alison] was sixteen years of age.

[Alison] advised this continued to escalate during two years. The routine became familiar to [Alison]. Epstein's assistant Sarah would telephone her every time Epstein was in the Town of Palm Beach and would place appointments for her to visit and work for Epstein. Each time something new was introduced, additional monies were produced and offered for [Alison] to allow the acts to happen. [Alison] consented to perform all these acts but was adamant that there was an understanding with Epstein that no vaginal penetration would occur with his penis. [Alison] explained that Epstein's penis was deformed. [She] explained that his penis was oval shaped. [She] claimed when

Epstein's penis was erect, it was thick toward the bottom but was thin and small toward the head portion. [She] called Epstein's penis "egg-shaped." [She] stated Epstein would photograph Marcinkova and her naked and having sex and proudly display the photographs within the home. [Alison] stated during one visit to Epstein's house in which she provided a massage to Epstein, his female friend, Nada [sic] Marcinkova, was also present. [Alison] provided the massage in which Marcinkova and her would fondle each other's breasts and kiss for Epstein to enjoy. Towards the end of this massage, Epstein grabbed [Alison] and turned her over onto her stomach on the massage table and forcibly inserted his penis into her vagina: [Alison] stated Epstein began to pump his penis in her vagina. [She] became upset over this. She said her head was being held against the table forcibly, as he continued to pump inside her. She screamed "No!" and Epstein stopped. She told him that she did not want to have his penis inside of her. Epstein did not ejaculate inside of her and apologized for his actions and subsequently paid her a thousand dollars for that visit. [Alison] stated she knows he still displays her photographs through out the house.

What happened to Mary had been bad enough. But what happened to Alison was on a whole other level. She'd been caught with some pot, sure. But that was hardly a felony offense. It didn't make her a liar. And, in important respects, Alison's statement had aligned with Mary's and with statements they'd been given by other girls, including Wendy Dobbs. Could Wendy be trusted? Probably not. Almost certainly not. But again, what *she* said was also in line with what the police had heard from other girls.

Detective Recarey and his team had done exceptional work on the investigation that Officer Pagan had started.

It was enough, Reiter decided, to cause a judge to issue a search warrant.

CHAPTER 18

Michael Reiter: October 2005

On October 20, Palm Beach police officers execute a search warrant, signed by Judge Laura Johnson, at Jeffrey Epstein's home on El Brillo Way. Inside the house, an employee is on the phone with Epstein. They ask him, politely, to hang up. Then, guns drawn, they walk up the winding stairs to the home's second story.

Detective Recarey remains outside and reads the warrant, out loud, to Epstein's houseman while another officer videotapes them.

"This is your copy," Recarey says as he hands over the warrant. "When we are concluded, I will leave a list of what items we've taken, okay? I would ask that you don't answer your telephone. I know that the gentleman was having a conversation with Mr. Epstein at the time. So I'm sure he's trying to call and find out what's going on. He will be told what was going on as soon as we're done. Okay?"

Inside the house, detectives see the pink-and-green couch that Mary and other girls had described. They see photos of naked young girls—in some cases, girls they've spoken to about Epstein. They also find message pads on which are written first names, dates, and numbers for the girls.

Sometimes there are notes to go with the names and numbers: "I have girls for him." Or "I have 2 girls for him."

These notes are signed by one Sarah Kellen.

Epstein's house has a strangely antiseptic quality. Some of the bedrooms look almost like doctors' offices. In the bathroom off Epstein's bedroom, there's a massage table as well as stands holding strange machines, which looked like something you'd find in a dermatologist's office.

In a wood-colored armoire beside Epstein's bed, they see a bottle of peach-flavored Joy Jelly. In the bathroom, there are soaps shaped like penises and vaginas, bottles of Mango Mist, more Joy Jelly, and boxes of tampons.

The officers find stacks of UFC videos and DVDs of *Rock Star* and other B-list movies.

They also find receipts for books bought on Amazon, such as *SlaveCraft: Roadmaps for Erotic Servitude*.

On the first floor, detectives are drawn to two secret cameras hidden in clocks. On the computer hard drive, they see several photographs of Wendy and other girls. These images appear to come from the camera inside the clock behind Epstein's desk.

The officers know where the cameras are because they helped install them—in 2004, when Epstein complained that someone had stolen a gun and $2,700 from him. Detective Recarey had investigated that case. But before he could arrest Epstein's handyman, Juan Alessi, for the theft, Epstein contacted a captain in the Palm Beach PD and prevailed upon him to have the investigation called off.

Epstein had met Alessi at a luncheonette, he explained, and Alessi had agreed to pay back the money. At the time, it made no sense to prosecute: Epstein was a busy man. He was going to get his money. But he did invite the police into his home to install the cameras. This was a service that the Palm Beach PD provided (though Epstein would be the only one with access to the footage). But while they were there, the police had noticed a group of attractive young women who seemed to be camped out at the house.

The group included Sarah Kellen and Nadia Marcinkova.

None of the girls was a relative of Epstein—that fact had caught the cops' attention.

And now, as the search continues, the cops see photographs of the very same girls.

On Epstein's desk, the officers find Alison's high school transcript.

The thing is, the detectives can't shake the feeling that the Epstein house has been tidied up for their arrival. Shelves look as though they've been emptied, and several photographs appear to have been removed from the walls.

"[Judging] by the condition of the place to be searched," Chief Reiter will say in his deposition for *B.B. vs. Epstein,* "someone probably had cleaned it up a bit."

Maybe there's nothing *too* surprising about this. After all, Reiter's team knows that Epstein's gotten wind of their investigation. What *is* surprising is that for a house that's been scrubbed, there's so much left lying around.

In fact, the oddest thing about the search is that someone appears to have gone through the house, gotten rid of incriminating materials, but left *many* clues behind.

It was as if the things the police were seeing didn't even register as wrong.

There's another feeling the cops can't shake: the nagging sense that they themselves are being investigated and tailed.

First Reiter hears through the grapevine that Epstein's lawyers have hired private investigators to perform background checks.

A public-records demand has been filed in an effort to obtain Reiter's own records.

Detective Recarey tells Reiter that he, too, is being surveilled and that his trash has been picked through.

In his entire career as a police officer, this is the first time that Reiter's seen or heard of such a thing: a suspect investigating his investigators. But for the moment, he puts it aside. Recarey's doing great work on the investigation. He's deeply invested, and for good reason: the detective's got four kids of his own. Right now, more victims are coming out of the woodwork. And now that the warrant's been executed, there's no downside to interviewing Epstein's servants.

CHAPTER 19

Detective Recarey, Probable-Cause Affidavit:
May 2006

> *On November 21, 2005 I interviewed Jose [sic] Alessi,*
> *a former houseman for Jeffrey Epstein. Alessi stated*
> *he was employed for eleven years with Mr. Epstein,*
> *from approximately 1993 through 2004. Alessi stated*
> *he was the house manager, driver and house mainte-*
> *nance person. It was his responsibility to prepare the*
> *house for Epstein's arrival. When asked about cooks*
> *or assistants, Alessi stated they traveled with Epstein*
> *on his private plane. I asked Mr. Alessi about the*
> *massages that have occurred at Epstein's home. Alessi*
> *stated Epstein receives three massages a day. Each*
> *masseuse that visited the house was different. Alessi*
> *stated that towards the end of his employment, the*
> *masseuses were younger and younger. When asked*
> *how young, Mr. Alessi stated they appeared to be six-*
> *teen or seventeen years of age at the most. The mas-*
> *sages would occur in Epstein's bedroom or bathroom.*
> *He knew this because he often set up the massage*
> *tables. I asked if there were things going on other than*

a massage. Alessi stated that there were times towards the end of his employment that he would have to wash off a massager/vibrator and a long rubber penis, which were in the sink after the massage. Additionally, he stated the bed would almost always have to be made after the massage.

On January 4, 2006 I interviewed another former houseman, Mr. Alfredo Rodriguez. During a sworn taped statement, Mr. Rodriguez stated he was employed by Jeffrey Epstein for approximately six months, from November 2004 through May of 2005. His responsibilities as house manager included being the butler, chauffeur, chef, houseman [and to] run errands for Epstein and provide for Epstein's guests. I asked Rodriguez about masseuses coming to the house. Rodriguez stated Epstein would have two massages a day. Epstein would have one massage in the morning and one massage in the afternoon everyday he was in residence. Rodriguez stated he would be informed to expect someone and make them comfortable until either Sarah Kellen or Epstein would meet with them. Rodriguez stated once the masseuses would arrive, he would allow them entry into the kitchen area and offer them something to drink or eat. They would then be encountered by either Sarah Kellen or Epstein. They would be taken upstairs to provide the massage. I asked Rodriguez if any of the masseuses appeared young in age. Rodriguez stated the girls that would come appeared to be too young to be masseuses. He stated one time under Epstein's direction, he delivered a dozen roses to [Mary's high school] for one of the girls that came to provide a massage. He knew the girls were still in high school and were of high school age. I asked Rodriguez about the massages. He felt there was a lot more going on than just massages.

*He would often clean Mr. Epstein's bedroom after
the alleged massages and would discover massagers/
vibrators and sex toys scattered on the floor. He also
said he would wipe down the vibrators and sex toys
and put them away in an armoire. He described the
armoire as a small wood armoire which was on the
wall close to Epstein's bed. On one occasion Epstein
ordered Rodriguez to go to the Dollar rent a car and
rent a car for the same girl he brought the roses to, so
that she could drive her self to Epstein's house without
incident. Rodriguez said the girl always needed rides
to and from the house.*

*Rodriguez produced a green folder which con-
tained documents, and a note with Mr. Epstein's
stationery with direction to deliver a bucket of roses
to [Mary's] High School after [a] high school drama
performance....*

*During the course of the investigation, subpoenas
were obtained for cell phone and home phone records
from several victims and witnesses along with the cell
phone records of Sarah Kellen. An analysis of these
records was conducted which found numerous telephone calls were made between Sarah Kellen and
the victims. These records indicate the dates the calls
were made are consistent with the dates and times the
victims/witnesses stated they were contacted. Specifically, the phone records showed Kellen called [Wendy
Dobbs] during the exact times and dates when [name
redacted] advised the incident occurred. Kellen also
coordinated the encounters with [name redacted]
during the time frame the girls stated they occurred.*

*Pursuant to a lawful subpoena I obtained Epstein's
private plane records for 2005 from Jet Aviation. The
plane records show arrival and departure of Epstein's
plane at Palm Beach International airport. These*

*records were compared to the cell phone records of
Sarah Kellen. This comparison found that all the
phone calls Kellen made to [Dobbs] and the victims
were made in the days just prior to their arrival or
during the time Epstein was in Palm Beach.*

*Therefore, as Jeffrey Epstein, who at the time of
these incidents was fifty one years of age, did have vaginal intercourse either with his penis or digitally with
[names redacted], who were minors at the time this
occurred, there is sufficient probable cause to charge
Jeffrey Epstein with four counts of Unlawful Sexual
Activity with a Minor, in violation of Florida State
Statute 794.05(1), a second degree felony. As Epstein,
who at the time of the incident was fifty two years of
age, did use a vibrator on the external vaginal area
of [name redacted], a fourteen year old minor, there
is sufficient probable cause to charge him with Lewd
and Lascivious Molestation, in violation of Florida
State Statute 800.04 (5), a second degree felony.*

PART II

The Man

CHAPTER 20

Jeffrey Epstein: 1953–1969

Jeffrey Epstein's mother, Paula, was the daughter of Max and Lena Stolofsky, who arrived in the United States as Lithuanian refugees. Relatives on that side of the family who remained in the old country would all perish in the course of Adolf Hitler's campaign to exterminate European Jewry.

Epstein's father, Seymour, was a manual laborer, like his father before him. Seymour's parents, Julius and Bessie Epstein, had emigrated from Russia and landed in Brooklyn, both of them with eighth-grade educations. They lived in Crown Heights, where Julius owned a house-wrecking company.

Before landing a job with the city, Seymour had worked with his father.

They were kind people, says Epstein's childhood friend Gary Grossberg. Seymour was there for him at a difficult time, Grossberg says. When Grossberg was young, his parents divorced, and his father moved out of Brooklyn. Seymour and Paula took Gary in. Often they referred to him as their third son. "Paula was a wonderful mother and homemaker," Grossberg remembers, "despite the fact that she had a full-time job."

Epstein, as a kid, was "chubby, with curly hair and a high, 'hee-hee' kind of laugh," Beverly Donatelli recalls.* Beverly was two years older than Epstein, but thanks to his precocious talents, which allowed him to skip two grades, they graduated from Brooklyn's Lafayette High School together, in 1969.

"He was *advanced*," Beverly remembers. "He tutored my girlfriend and myself in the summer. He taught me geometry in *just two months*."

When Beverly thinks of Epstein now, she recalls gentler times—long strolls down the Coney Island boardwalk, roller-coaster rides, stolen kisses. "That last year in school, I think he kind of loved me," she says. "One night on the beach he kissed me. In fact, our history teacher made up a mock wedding invitation for Jeffrey and myself to show to the class. That seems pretty inappropriate now. But back then, we all thought it was funny. Jews and the Italians, that was pretty much who went to Lafayette High School. They didn't socialize that much. And though my mother was crazy about him, she told me Jewish boys don't marry Italians."

Through the haze of several decades, Beverly remembers Epstein as a kindhearted boy and something of a prodigy—a gifted young pianist as well as a math whiz.

"I was talking to my girlfriends the other day," she says. "There is nothing but nice we can say about him. He is actually the reason I went to college."

Beverly lost contact with Epstein over the years. But not long after Epstein's fiftieth birthday, she got a call out of the blue.

---

* Beverly Donatelli's name, some identifying details, and dialogue have been changed.

"He had a photo of us on the beach," she says. "A friend noticed it at his birthday party. And Jeffrey said to the friend: 'I bet she has a big ass now.' So Jeffrey called me and invited me to his home on 71st Street. We hung out. We reminisced. He was the same Jeffrey. A gentleman."

The two never did speak again, but to this day Beverly sympathizes with her high school sweetheart.

"I feel so bad for him," Beverly says. "That's how much I liked him."

Gary Grossberg was a year younger than Epstein and in the same class as Epstein's kid brother, Mark, with whom Grossberg remains very friendly, though he hasn't seen or spoken with Jeffrey in some time. Both brothers are good people, he says.

"Jeffrey's a brilliant and good person. He is also incredibly generous."

Grossberg says he's talked to Epstein about "the problem in Florida." As he sees it, Epstein "got carried away... perhaps he was hanging around with the wrong people."

Grossberg wonders, too, if the things that made Epstein special contributed to his eventual fall from grace.

"He was a diamond in the rough, you see," Grossberg explains. "People recognized Jeffrey's brilliance very early on. But he had a gift for recognizing opportunities very quickly. He started buying properties in Manhattan, including 301 East 66th Street. He asked his brother—did Mark want to join him? He did."

Grossberg himself has had his ups and downs. At one point, he worked in a building owned by the Epstein brothers. There, he says, a porter told him a story about a little-known side of Jeffrey Epstein. The porter's wife, who lived in South America, desperately needed an organ transplant. Epstein paid for the operation.

"That's just typical," Grossberg says. "That's who he always was, long as I knew him."

"Lafayette was a city school," says another old classmate, James Rosen. "It was functional. There was nothing special about it."

James Rosen is a retired postal worker. He lives in South Florida now, but, like Jeffrey Epstein, he'd grown up in Sea Gate.

"There was a lot of volatility at Lafayette," Rosen recalls. "It was a blue-collar area that was, at one time, 90 percent Italian. Then a small amount of Jews moved in, and there was anti-Semitism. The Italians didn't want the Jews to be there."

Black families were moving in, too, he remembers, and Hispanic ones. But he says most of the animosity was aimed at Jews.

"There were fights in the schools. They thought we were going to take over."

But Epstein seems to have made friends easily. Even then, his buddies—who called him Eppy—could see he was special. While they hung out on the beach, Epstein played the piano. Did homework. Worked on his prized stamp collection.

Innocent times.

CHAPTER 21

Jeffrey Epstein: 1969–1976

It's the height of the Vietnam War. Students collide
with college administrators. Hippies collide with
hard hats. Kids with long hair collide with their parents. Jeffrey Epstein does not go in for any of that. At
the age of sixteen, he's taking advanced math classes at
Cooper Union, an august institution in the East Village
where Abraham Lincoln once spoke.

Thanks to a generous endowment, the school is
tuition free, though the application process is famously
rigorous.

Epstein sails through it.

At Harvard or Yale, his accent would give him away.
Epstein *tawks* like the Brooklyn boy he is. But Cooper
Union is more open than any Ivy League school. It's full
of boys from Brooklyn, and, aside from his prodigious
intellect, Epstein doesn't stand out. He starts to make
money by tutoring his fellow students. And in 1971, he
leaves Cooper Union for the greener pastures of New
York University, located a few blocks away. There, at the
Courant Institute of Mathematical Sciences, he studies

the mathematical physiology of the heart. But he never graduates from any college or university.

By 1973, Epstein is teaching at the Dalton School, a prestigious private school on the Upper East Side. Like Tavern on the Green, Grand Central Terminal, and the Century Association, Dalton is a New York institution— an elite K–12 rocket ship built for the children of New York's ruling classes.

It's not at all clear how Epstein, who has no college degree, ends up there.

And yet here he is, barely out of his teens and already a teacher of math and physics. "Go forth unafraid" is the Dalton School's credo.

It's a philosophy Epstein has adopted. For him, Dalton's an excellent launching pad.

It's nothing like Lafayette High School. The kids he's teaching are rich—very rich. Their parents are extremely well connected. And despite Epstein's outer-borough accent, he's careful in his presentation. At any given moment, he's one parent-teacher conference away from a whole new world of possibilities.

Because Dalton has an excellent student-to-teacher ratio, the parents get to know Epstein quite well. Before long, a Wall Street *macher* named Alan "Ace" Greenberg has taken a special shine to the young man who's been tutoring his son Ted.

Like Epstein, Ace Greenberg came from a humble background.

The son of an Oklahoma City shopkeeper, he won a football scholarship to the University of Oklahoma, transferred to the University of Missouri following a back injury, and graduated in 1949. That same year, he moved to New York and, after a series of rejections at white-shoe firms—places that never would hire a Jew—landed a job at Bear Stearns, earning $32.50 a week as a clerk.

By 1958, he'd been made a full partner. Built like a pit bull, Greenberg smoked cigars, performed coin tricks for his friends, and always dressed in a bow tie. He was an all-elbows trader—gruff, cheap, and, above all, impatient. He was also a champion bridge player, a hunter of big game in Africa, and the firm but loyal leader of the team he'd built at Bear Stearns—an unusual team made up mostly of men who'd grown up in New York's outer boroughs.

Greenberg didn't care about MBAs or Ivy League diplomas. What he cared about was raw talent and drive. Greenberg cultivated risk takers, unconventional thinkers, and he looked high (and especially low) for his "PSDs": men who, in his estimation, were poor, smart, and, above all, determined.

Jeffrey Epstein, the Dalton School teacher, fit Greenberg's bill perfectly.

CHAPTER 22

Jeffrey Epstein: 1976–1981

According to several published reports, it was Ace Greenberg's son, Ted, who introduced Epstein to Greenberg. But other sources say Greenberg's daughter, Lynne, was dating Epstein at the time. According to them, *that* was how Epstein got into Bear Stearns—by charming a young and beautiful woman and using her to advance his career.

At Bear Stearns, Epstein started as an assistant to a trader on the American Stock Exchange and quickly worked up to junior partner, which meant that he was entitled to a share of the profits. Still in his twenties, he was running with the bulls, kicking down any doors that stood in his way.

The view from Ace Greenberg's office, high above Madison Avenue in midtown, was striking. At night, the whole city was lit up like a stage set.

It was Epstein's city now, to win or to lose. And there were women to go with the prize. Tall, beautiful women, blondes and brunettes, who wouldn't have given a math teacher the time of day. Now they found Epstein exciting and *handsome*.

Greenberg's gorgeous assistant was one of these women.

If Greenberg knew about their affair, he did not seem to care. Then again, Greenberg had other things on his mind. The Reagan era, when deregulation kicked into high gear, was still on the horizon. But there was already a decreasing amount of government oversight on Wall Street, and a new breed of bare-knuckle traders had begun to push every available limit. It was the start of the age of corporate raiders, and with Ace Greenberg looking out for him, Epstein had no reservations when it came to throwing his weight around. The golden boy's gift for working the numbers earned him a place in the special-products division, where he worked on extremely complex tax-related problems for a select group of Bear Stearns's wealthiest clients—an elite within the elite—including Seagram CEO Edgar Bronfman.

In the spring of 1981 Bronfman made a bid to take over the St. Joe Minerals Corporation. He offered forty-five dollars a share, or close to three times the value of St. Joe's stock. The whole offer amounted to $2.1 billion in cash.

But St. Joe's executives didn't want to sell their 118-year-old company. In a press release, they called Seagram's bid unsolicited and dismissed it as "grossly inadequate." At which point the SEC decided to investigate.

There were allegations of insider trading. Within a few weeks, Bear Stearns's employees were called in to testify.

Epstein got called in as well and categorically denied any wrongdoing.

But, as it turned out, he'd just resigned from Bear Stearns.

CHAPTER 23

Jeffrey Epstein: 1981

Epstein will always maintain that his resignation had nothing to do with the SEC's investigation into Bear Stearns and Edgar Bronfman's ill-fated attempt to take over St. Joe's.

But of course this raises the question: Why *did* Epstein resign from Bear Stearns?

In his testimony before the SEC, Epstein says he was offended by the company's investigation of a twenty-thousand-dollar loan he'd made to his friend Warren Eisenstein. Epstein didn't know it at the time, he maintains, but if used to buy stock, such a loan might have been unethical, if not illegal.

On top of that, questions about Epstein's expenses had come up.

In the end, Bear Stearns fined him $2,500—an embarrassing thing, to be sure. So much for making full partner anytime soon.

But $2,500 is not $250,000 or even $25,000. Who'd give up a job as junior partner over that?

Another one of Epstein's bosses, James "Jimmy" Cayne, will say, "Jeffrey Epstein left Bear of his own volition." Epstein wanted to strike out on his own, Cayne explains. But given the timing, some questions remain. Then there's Epstein's own testimony, given on April 1, 1981, before SEC investigators Jonathan Harris and Robert Blackburn:

Q: Sir, are you aware that certain rumors may have been circulating around your firm in connection with your reasons for leaving the firm?
A: I'm aware that there were many rumors.
Q: What rumors have you heard?
A: Nothing to do with St. Joe.
Q: Can you relate what you heard?
A: It was having to do with an illicit affair with a secretary.

As far as the investigators are concerned, this is new information; the first time a secretary's name has come up. But they have no interest in Epstein's office romance and press on:

Q: Mr. Epstein, did anyone at Bear Stearns tell you in words or substance that you should not divulge anything about St. Joe Minerals to the staff of the Securities and Exchange Commission? Has anyone indicated to you in any way, either directly or indirectly, in words or substance, that your compensation for this past year or any future monies coming to you from Bear Stearns will be contingent upon your not divulging information to the Securities and Exchange Commission?
A: No.

* * *

Whatever the reasons for his resignation, Epstein still gets his annual bonus of around $100,000 (roughly $275,000 in today's dollars). The SEC never brings charges against him or any other Bear Stearns employee. And so the particulars of Epstein's departure get folded up into the greater mystery surrounding the man. Did Epstein crash the rocket ship that Ace Greenberg had given him to pilot? Or did he take it and fly it out, over the horizon?

Either way, Epstein was out on his own.

For him, the future would only get brighter.

CHAPTER 24

Ana Obregón: 1982

Ana Obregón was one of the world's most beautiful women and well on her way to becoming famous as such when she first met Jeffrey Epstein. For her, there would be film roles—in the 1984 Bo Derek vehicle *Bolero,* Ana Obregón gives the star a run for her money—and appearances on the covers of Spanish *Playboy* and Spanish *Vanity Fair.*

As for fortune, Obregón had that already.

Ana's father was a very wealthy investor in Spain. But he also had serious problems. On June 15, 1982, a venerable stock- and bond-trading firm, the Drysdale Securities Corporation, announced that it was going out of business. Just that year, Drysdale had spun off a subsidiary operation called Drysdale Government Securities. And in May, DGS defaulted on $160 million in interest payments it owed on Treasury securities that it had borrowed. In doing so, DGS had dragged down its parent company.

A very well-connected group of Spanish families— including members of Spain's royal family—had invested with Drysdale. Those investors stood to lose hundreds of millions of dollars. And Ana's father was one of those investors.

What Ana wanted from Jeffrey Epstein was help in recovering her father's money.

"My father, he's done something stupid," she told him.

A Spanish accent. A Brooklyn accent. They blended well together, and Ana was so very lovely.

It turned out that Epstein was willing to help.

"Something stupid, you see, with the money. The family money. Some—what do you call it? A scheme. He knew some of the people, but they lied to him. And now the money is gone."

People who knew Jeffrey Epstein recall that he was bad off after his exit or ouster—whatever it was—from Bear Stearns. Moving from couch to couch for a while. Sleeping in his lawyer's offices before settling down in an apartment in the Solow Tower, on East 66th Street.

It's a bit hard to believe. After all, Epstein left Bear Stearns with a good deal of money. But Epstein's lifestyle was expensive. He was a man on the make then, and Ana was still in her twenties, plying her craft at the Actors Studio—the New York City theater institution that Marlon Brando, Robert De Niro, Jack Nicholson, and Jane Fonda had all been members of.

Epstein told Ana that he'd formed a company, International Assets Group.

To Ana, this sounded very impressive. In fact, IAG was a small operation that Epstein was running out of his apartment. But if Ana had known that, would she have cared? She could already see that Epstein was brilliant. And though she would maintain that their friendship was strictly platonic, it was Ana who helped set Epstein on his course. Like other beautiful women he'd cultivate throughout his life, she opened doors to whole other kingdoms.

Ones that no boys from Brooklyn had even dreamed of.

Andrew Levander was an assistant US attorney in the Southern District of New York's Securities and Commodities Fraud Task Force. He was assigned to look into Drysdale's collapse. The case he was building would result in fraud convictions for a number of Drysdale executives, and even today, Levander remembers Epstein bringing "a very attractive woman" to meet him when Epstein came to him in the course of the investigation.

The woman was Ana Obregón.

Levander told Ana that he was already working the case. A lawyer named Robert Gold, who was a former federal prosecutor himself, was assisting. And now Epstein would join them in the hunt for the monies.

In effect, DGS had built a series of labyrinths, rabbit holes, deadfalls. And even investors who'd lost vast sums to the company were less than forthcoming when it came to speaking to the US attorney. Several of the investors were foreign. Some had violated their own countries' laws pertaining to foreign investments.

This was where Epstein—with his calm, confident air of discretion—came in.

Ana Obregón gave Epstein power of attorney over any monies that he recovered. And though it took him three years, working with Robert Gold and the US attorney's office, Epstein finally did make his way to the center of DGS's maze and recover Obregón's money.

Most of it was being held in a bank in the Cayman Islands.

Epstein's agreement with Ana prevents us from knowing how much he recovered—and how much he kept.

But given the amounts at stake, Epstein likely earned millions—or more—and to this day Ana Obregón has nothing but appreciation for what Epstein accomplished.

"I know he's had some problems," she says. "I don't want anything to do with that."

As for Epstein, he came out of the deal with a new modus operandi: from now on, he'd only work with the super rich.

CHAPTER 25

Eva Andersson: July 8, 1980

Miss Sweden, Eva Birgitta Andersson, is wearing a dazzling white gown and sweating, ever so slightly, under the stage lights. But Bob Barker's about to announce the winner of this, the twenty-ninth Miss Universe pageant, held in Seoul, South Korea, and Eva's smile is as wide as the ocean.

"And now that we know what Miss Universe will win, let's see which five girls are still in the running!"

Barker pauses, like the expert broadcaster he is. Eva's chest tightens. There are twelve women on stage, all of them beautiful—even if they're not quite as beautiful as Miss Sweden.

"On this card are the names of five contestants who have received the highest total score from our judges in the personal interview, the swimsuit, and the evening gown competition."

Eva feels the camera pan across the stage—pan across *her,* standing in between Miss Scotland and Miss Puerto Rico.

"As a result, they will be our five finalists. As I call

each name, you will see a figure on your television screen. That is the total score received by the contestant since she became a semifinalist. But one thing I would point out to you: the point total is not necessarily a sign of who our eventual winner will be. Being first now is no guarantee of being first at the time of our judges' final ballot."

Oh, get on with it, Miss Sweden thinks. And, as if by her command, Bob Barker does.

"Now our five finalists. Good luck, girls! The first finalist is: *Miss Sweden!*"

Eva's hands fly up to her face. The time it takes her to walk to the front of the stage is all the time she needs to stop herself from crying.

For Eva, it's not meant to be. Miss USA, Shawn Weatherly, wins that year's competition—she'll go on to become a star on *Baywatch*. But Eva's future is secure nonetheless. After the pageant, she'll spend three years studying in Stockholm, finish med school at UCLA, and become a doctor of internal medicine.

Along the way, she'll meet Jeffrey Epstein.

People who knew them when they were a couple say that Eva wanted to marry Epstein. One friend says he considered it seriously. In the end, Eva ended up with a man named Glenn Dubin, though she and Epstein remained very close. And if Eva was the proverbial "one who got away," Epstein ended up dating other impressive women—world-class beauties—as he made his way in the world.

Why didn't any of the romances take? Perhaps there was always someone more fabulous waiting for Epstein around the corner. Perhaps none of these women satisfied Epstein's deeper urges. But he did have a knack for keeping the women he'd dated by his side through thick and thin, long after he'd broken up with them.

When he was through with his girlfriends, Epstein would say, they graduated up, not down, the ladder, moving from the status of "lover" to "friend."

In his estimation, these shifts always constituted a promotion.

The world was full of beautiful women. But for Epstein, friendship seemed to be a far more precious commodity.

CHAPTER 26

Jeffrey Epstein: 1984

How *did* Jeffrey Epstein make all his money?

Epstein would tell stories over the years about monies recovered from slippery characters. Sometimes, friends and former associates would say, he'd suggest he had ties to the government, giving listeners the impression that he was doing dangerous, glamorous work.

Others said that what Epstein *really* did, at this stage in his career, was much more banal. According to them, Epstein spent most of his time coming up with creative new ways for the rich to avoid paying taxes. The commission for tax-avoidance deals was enormous, although the number of deals Epstein was involved with is a matter of conjecture, as is his record of successes and failures.

But Epstein's business model was evolving. He'd charge a flat fee. No fancy math. No percentages.

Pay me fifty million dollars. Or pay the IRS seven times that amount.

At first Epstein did not demand his fee up front. Instead he asked that the payment—often a substantial one—be put into escrow. If his strategy worked, he'd get paid. If not, the money bounced back to the client.

In the eighties, when tax rates on the top 1 percent were much, much higher than they are today, topping out at close to 50 percent, it was an extremely effective pitch. And then there were other ways to make money.

In 1982, Epstein sold his wealthy friends, his friends' wealthy relatives, and others on an oil-drilling deal. One of the investors, Michael Stroll, had run Williams Electronics, an entertainment company known for the pinball machines it made.

Stroll put $450,000 into the oil deal.

But in 1984, Michael Stroll wanted his money back. Despite repeated demands and requests for a full accounting of what Epstein owed him, he got $10,000 back on his $450,000 investment. Eventually he sued Epstein in federal court for the remaining $440,000— the case went on for a number of years. In court, Epstein told the judge that the $10,000 he'd returned was actually the payment for a horse Stroll had sold him.

Like many cases involving Epstein, this one was settled out of court, the terms of the final agreement kept secret.

CHAPTER 27

Steven Hoffenberg: July 10, 1987

Before there was Bernie Madoff, there was Steven Hoffenberg.

In 1987, Hoffenberg was the head of Towers Financial Corporation, a company that bought debts, such as unpaid medical bills, at a very steep discount while pressing the debtors to repay in full. He'd started the company fifteen years earlier with two thousand dollars and just a handful of employees. Thanks, in part, to a grueling work ethic, he'd turned that into a much bigger concern, with twelve hundred employees and stock that traded over the counter. But Hoffenberg still spent fifteen hours each day, six days a week, in his office.

He wanted more. Hoffenberg was a Wall Street outsider. A Brooklyn boy. A college dropout, like Epstein.

One thing Hoffenberg wanted was respect. The other was someone who was familiar with Wall Street's inner workings. Jeffrey Epstein, who had traded options for Bear Stearns, fit the bill.

Hoffenberg began paying twenty-five thousand dollars per month for Epstein's expertise as a consultant.

The SEC had already looked into Hoffenberg's affairs, settling with him out of court in a matter relating to unregistered securities. But Hoffenberg was dangling a very big prize.

In the 1980s, several major financial players were involved in the greenmailing of publicly traded companies. What greenmailing means, in practice, is that a brokerage house or group of investors will start buying shares in companies that seem to be vulnerable to takeover attempts. To ward off the attempts, executives at those companies will buy the shares back at a premium. It's risky, but very often the investors stand to make a handsome profit.

Yet another thing Hoffenberg wanted was to take over Pan American World Airways. The iconic airline had already entered its downward trajectory, but it was still a giant.

For Hoffenberg, the greenmailing profits could have been huge.

According to Hoffenberg, Epstein handled the attempted takeover of Pan Am—a deal that went sideways almost immediately.

Steven Hoffenberg still has a lot to say on the subject. But in listening to him, one must bear in mind that in 1995, he pleaded guilty to criminal conspiracy and fraud charges involving a $460 million swindle, a familiar scheme to anyone who followed the Bernie Madoff case.

Like so many others, Hoffenberg had tried to fly very high without the necessary updraft. And despite all the hours he spent at the office, he'd also developed a taste for the high life. He bought his own jet, a luxury yacht, and a Long Island mansion to go with his expensive Manhattan apartment. He'd also briefly owned a controlling interest in the *New York Post*.

To cover his tracks, Hoffenberg had been taking money from investors and using it to pay previous investors. It was a classic Ponzi scheme—one of the biggest in history—and Hoffenberg ended up spending nineteen years in a federal prison.

Why was Epstein not implicated in the case? All that Hoffenberg will say when asked is: "Ask Robert Gold."

Another source suggests that Gold, the former federal prosecutor who had helped Epstein recover Ana Obregón's money, kept the US attorney away from Epstein until there were only a few weeks left before the statute of limitations ran out.

As for Epstein himself, he would always deny any wrongdoing. Despite his proximity to Hoffenberg, he managed to avoid the blast radius.

CHAPTER 28

Robert Meister: 1985

Robert Meister, the vice chairman of a giant insurance brokerage and consulting firm called Aon, met Jeffrey Epstein in the mid-eighties, aboard a flight from New York to Palm Beach. Both men were flying first class. Each one thought the other looked familiar. They talked in the course of that flight, and Meister filed the conversation away, only to recall it in 1989. At that time, Les Wexner, who was Meister's friend and a client of Meister's insurance company, was complaining to him about the people managing his money.

Wexner was a billionaire, but for all his wealth, his finances were in a tangle. Maybe Epstein could help. And perhaps Epstein would also be grateful for the introduction. Hard as it is to believe, there's evidence to suggest that Epstein really had spent the last of his last Bear Stearns bonus—along with his share of the money he'd recovered for Ana Obregón—and was broke, again, at the time.

One estranged friend says that he had to loan Epstein money to pay the bill at Epstein's garage, which had seized Epstein's car for nonpayment.

Another estranged friend says that Epstein didn't have two nickels to rub together.

Diana Crane, a former model, says that Epstein always had first-class upgrades he would give to his friends so they didn't have to fly economy class.

"No one knew where or how he got them," Crane recalls. "Sometimes they worked, and other times they didn't. I remember he saw a friend of mine wearing a Concorde jacket. He asked if he could borrow it for a day or so. My friend never got the jacket back. But Epstein would tell people he always flew on the Concorde—a *total* lie."

But even if Epstein were flush, Les Wexner would have been a big fish to catch.

From the get-go, Meister's wife, Wendy, had her suspicions about Epstein. About the way he presented himself and the way he worked himself into their inner circle.

Before long, Wendy was calling Epstein *the virus*.

But for Epstein, the Meisters weren't the point. Wexner was.

And hard as it is to understand why the billionaire would associate with a man who'd worked with a Ponzi king like Steven Hoffenberg, it turned out that Wexner and Epstein would get along perfectly well.

CHAPTER 29

Ghislaine Maxwell: 1991

Robert Meister was not the only friend who helped Jeffrey Epstein, the boy from Coney Island, on his way up the social ladder. There was also Ghislaine Maxwell, a wealthy heiress from the United Kingdom who'd retained her ties to some of the world's most glamorous and scandalous jet-setters.

Maxwell was the youngest and most favored child of one of the most famous—even infamous—men in Europe. Her father, Robert Maxwell, was a Czech refugee who had fought in the French Foreign Legion and with the British in World War II and had gone on to become a member of Parliament. By the 1960s, he'd become a media baron. Born into a Hasidic family—his birth name was Ján Ludvík Hyman Binyamin Hoch—Maxwell died in disgrace in 1991 after falling or perhaps jumping off the side of his supersize yacht, the *Lady Ghislaine*.

"The shtetl Solotvyno, where I come from, it is no more," Maxwell said a few months before his demise. "It was poor. It was Orthodox. And it was Jewish. We were very poor. We didn't have things that other people had. They had shoes, they had food, and we didn't. At the end of the war, I discovered the fate of my parents and my sisters and brothers, relatives, and neighbors. I don't know what went through their minds as they realized that they'd been tricked into a gas chamber."

Maxwell's own death was followed by an international scandal. It turned out that he'd stolen hundreds of millions of pounds from his companies' pension funds and used them to prop up his empire. Two of his sons were tried for conspiracy to commit fraud and ultimately exonerated. But Ghislaine, who had grown up in luxurious surroundings and counted the Duke of York, Prince Andrew, among her intimates, could not escape the dark shadow her father had cast. Looking to start fresh, she took the Concorde to New York City.

At first, it seems, Maxwell and Epstein were lovers. "She was madly in love with Jeffrey," says a longtime friend of Ghislaine's. Then they became something more. Ghislaine took care of Epstein's travel arrangements. She managed his household and opened doors that very few Brooklyn-born Jewish boys could have passed through. According to lawsuits and witness testimony, she also became one of several women who procured young girls for Epstein.

She was not jealous, according to people who knew her back then. If anything, Ghislaine seemed to take pleasure in satisfying Epstein's needs.

Ghislaine introduced Epstein to a fabulous world that the Brooklyn boy knew nothing about. One friend jokes that she taught Epstein the difference between a fish fork and a salad fork. But despite—or was it because of?—Maxwell's devotion to Epstein, she, too, graduated from girlfriend to friend status. According to *Jane Doe 102 vs. Jeffrey Epstein,* a civil complaint filed in 2009 by a woman later identified as Virginia Roberts, one of the services Maxwell provided for Epstein was the procurement of underage women. (Through her lawyer and in court papers, Maxwell has vehemently denied any involvement with Virginia, with any other young woman Epstein was involved with, or with any criminal activities committed by Jeffrey Epstein. In a 2016 answer to a defamation lawsuit brought by Roberts, Maxwell called the allegations fabricated for financial gain.)

The case of Nadia Bjorlin, who was thirteen when she was first noticed by Epstein, raises questions in this regard, at least in the eyes of her mother.

Bjorlin's Iranian-born mother spoke to a British tabloid some years ago about her family's disturbing experience with Maxwell and Epstein. Bjorlin's father, a celebrated conductor of classical music, had died a year earlier, the mother said. She believed that this made the girl a vulnerable and easy target.

"She was at school at the famed Interlochen Arts Center, in Michigan, when she met Epstein," the mother said.

"My daughter was a singer. She was a baby. She was a skinny little girl, not mature for her age. She was thirteen, but everyone thought she was nine or ten.

"Epstein was a big donor, and he heard about Nadia and that her father had died, so she was vulnerable, and he contacted her. He said, 'Here's my number.'

"He kept saying, 'Come—will you come?' He said he wanted to help mentor her. I wouldn't let her meet him. What sort of a man approaches a young girl and asks to meet her?"

In the meantime, Maxwell had become friendly with the family. "I trusted Ghislaine; she was like a mother,"

Bjorlin's mother recalled. "She was always calling my house.

"Ghislaine didn't want me to meet Epstein, but I did anyway, and I asked what he wanted with Nadia. He said he wanted to help her singing career. He said, 'I'd like to be like a godfather.' It felt creepy.

"I had a bad vibe about him and said, 'Stop!' I told him, 'No, thank you. She doesn't need your help.' I kept Nadia away from him. She never met him alone. She never went anywhere with him."

Despite her suspicions, it took Epstein's arrest to make Bjorlin's mother wonder whether Maxwell and Epstein hadn't been sizing her daughter up for his stable of underage women.

CHAPTER 30

Leslie Wexner: 1993

Leslie Wexner, the richest man in Ohio, is a proud midwesterner. Born into the rag trade (Wexner's parents were Russian-Jewish immigrants), he grew up to be a straight shooter—taciturn and camera-shy.

For several years running, his 315-foot boat, the *Limitless,* was the largest yacht owned by an American.

Wexner's employees loved him, and he was known to be fiercely loyal to them.

In time, he'd come to see the same qualities in Jeffrey Epstein.

"Everyone was mystified as to what [Epstein's] appeal was," says Robert Morosky, a former vice chairman of the clothing retailer the Limited, founded by Wexner.

"Almost everyone at the Limited wondered who he was," another former employee of Wexner's recalls. "He literally came out of nowhere."

But it seems that Epstein did work hard to untangle Wexner's finances. And it appears he succeeded. "Jeffrey cleaned that up right away," a former associate of Epstein's says.

The two men became all but inseparable.

"Very smart, with a combination of excellent judgment and unusually high standards," Wexner said of Epstein at the time. "Also, he is always a most loyal friend."

When Wexner wanted to break up with a woman he'd been dating for several years—a woman who moved to Ohio and converted to Judaism to make him happy—he dispatched Epstein to do the dirty work.

When Wexner hired a decorator for his Ohio mansion and wanted someone to verify the authenticity of several expensive antiques, Epstein flew in his friend Stuart Pivar, the renowned art collector and author. (According to Pivar, most of the antiques were cheap imitations.) When Wexner traveled abroad, he'd bring back trinkets and gifts for Epstein. When Wexner wanted to see *Cats,* Epstein arranged to have the cast perform in his mansion.

In Ohio, Wexner's associates whispered about his relationship with Jeffrey Epstein. In New York, they wondered about Epstein's role in Wexner's 1993 marriage to Abigail Koppel.

At thirty-one, Koppel was twenty-four years Wexner's junior. It was Epstein who negotiated the prenuptial agreement and orchestrated its very strange signing. Abigail signed the agreement in her law office. Wexner signed it in his office. According to an associate of Epstein's who was present, Epstein brought a *Sports Illustrated* swimsuit model along to Wexner's office, as if to make the point that there are other beautiful women in the world. As a joke, Epstein placed the agreement on the model's belly and had Wexner sign it right there.

Epstein asked his friend: "Are you sure you want to do this?"

"Yes, Jeffrey," said Wexner. "Quite sure."

"It was an uproarious scene," Epstein's associate recalls. "Just Jeffrey being Jeffrey. That was his gestalt."

PART III
The Women

CHAPTER 31

Mc2 Model Management's NYC branch is looking for "highly motivated and energetic" interns to assist their agents part-time or full-time. If you're thinking to yourself, who?, it's the agency founded by Jean-Luc Brunel, the guy who first signed Christy Turlington when she was just fourteen. Responsibilities include scanning pictures, answering phones, assisting with updating models' portfolios, and working in Photoshop, Word and Excel (so you have to already know what you're doing in those). You Must: Be interested in the fashion, modeling and photography industries, outgoing, well spoken, and able to keep cool while five different people demand Starbucks / copies / phone calls / etc. This is a great opportunity to get hands-on experience at a smaller agency, plus they can offer a stipend and a Metrocard as well as school credit if needed. Send your resume to intern@mc2mm.com Good luck!

—Julia Hermanns, *Fashionista,*
January 30, 2009

Jean-Luc Brunel: 2005

For Jeffrey Epstein, Leslie Wexner is more than a mentor. More than the last in a line of older men—father figures—whom Epstein cultivated while making his way in the world.

Wexner is also a steady, if indirect, source of beautiful women.

After all, Wexner is the man in charge of Victoria's Secret, part of the Limited family of companies and—better yet—in charge of the Victoria's Secret catalog. What this means for Epstein is models galore. In fact, like a fox that's gotten hold of the lease to a henhouse, Epstein, according to evidence collected in a later lawsuit brought by Epstein victims, eventually provided financial support for a modeling agency, and provided support for models employed by that agency, in New York City.

This story begins with a Frenchman—a playboy modeling agent named Jean-Luc Brunel—who was an owner of the Karin modeling agency.

Brunel had been working as a modeling agent since the seventies. He claimed to have launched the careers of Monica Bellucci, Estelle, Jerry Hall, Rachel Hunter, Milla Jovovich, Rebecca Romijn, Kristina Semenovskaya, Sharon Stone, and Estella Warren, as well as Christy Turlington and other well-known cover girls. Brunel had also been a subject of a *60 Minutes* investigation, broadcast in 1988, into sexual exploitation in the modeling industry. That exposé had caused Eileen Ford of the elite Ford modeling agency to sever her ties with the playboy. (Brunel's activities were also chronicled in a 1995 book about the fashion industry—*Model: The Ugly Business of Beautiful Women,* by Michael Gross.)

But Brunel's reputation did not prevent Jeffrey Epstein from getting involved in his business.

According to a summary judgment court filing by Bradley Edwards, a victims' lawyer defending against a lawsuit by Jeffrey Epstein alleging fabrication of sexual assault cases against him, Epstein had provided support for Brunel's agency, which changed its name, in 2005, from Karin to MC2—as in $E = mc^2$.

As a scout for MC2, Brunel traveled the world in search of undiscovered talent, favoring Scandinavia, Israel, central Europe, the former Soviet republics, and South America, setting up modeling competitions and negotiating with other international modeling agents and agencies.

But according to the court filing, in which Edwards detailed the information he had gathered in support of victims, Epstein and Brunel had used the agency to bring underage girls from foreign countries into the United States by promising them modeling contracts. These girls were then housed in condominiums belonging to Epstein. "Epstein and Brunel would then obtain a visa for these girls," the document states, "then charge the underage girls rent, presumably to live as underage prostitutes in the condos."

"I strongly deny having participated, neither directly nor indirectly, in the actions Mr. Jeffrey Epstein is being accused of," Brunel would say. "I strongly deny having committed any illicit act or any wrongdoing in the course of my work as a scouter or model agencies manager. I have exercised with the utmost ethical standard for almost forty years."

According to Brunel, his association with Jeffrey Epstein ended up having a strong negative impact on his reputation and business. Several photographers refused to work with him. Other agencies, such as Modilinos Model Management, curtailed their relationships with Brunel. And in 2015, Brunel filed his own civil lawsuit against Jeffrey Epstein, denying that he had any role in Epstein's illegal activities, alleging that Epstein had obstructed justice by telling him to avoid having his deposition taken in the criminal case the Palm Beach PD had built against Epstein, and claiming that false allegations of Brunel's links to Epstein's activities had harmed his reputation and cost him a great deal of business.

In his filing, Brunel included several e-mails from industry contacts who expressed their doubts about placing models with his agency. "Parents don't want their daughters coming to us because [when] they google your name and the agency name the only things they see is 'Sex Trafficking'!!!" one correspondent had written.

CHAPTER 32

Nadia Marcinkova: circa 2000

MC2 has offices in New York City. But Jeffrey's always *in motion*—flying to his homes in New Mexico and the Virgin Islands. Often to Palm Beach. Sometimes to Paris. And when he comes home to New York he hosts parties where important people—corporate titans, real estate tycoons, university presidents, Nobel Prize–winning scientists, princes, ex-presidents, and heads of state—mingle with beautiful women.

Some guests marvel in public: Who *are* these women? Where do they *come* from?

Nadia Marcinkova comes from Slovakia. She looks like a model. But Nadia's done very little modeling, if any. Instead she's become another of Epstein's girlfriends.

According to statements given to the Palm Beach police, she's also served as a willing accomplice in Epstein's sexual assaults on underage females.

Epstein prefers diminutive women, but Nadia is tall. She's rail-thin and blond like the sun, with glowing skin, a wide smile, and sky-high cheekbones.

On a good day, she could pass for a Bond girl—a

woman caught up in a web of crime and intrigue. But of course, that's exactly what she is.

In certain circles, the academics and the women in Epstein's orbit are almost a joke. In a 2003 profile of him, *New York* magazine quotes Harvard professors ("He is amazing"), Princeton professors ("He changed my life"), MIT professors ("If I had acted upon the investment advice he has given me over the years, I'd be calling you from my Gulfstream right now"), and other luminaries, up to and including Bill Clinton.

"I've known Jeff for fifteen years," says Donald Trump. "Terrific guy; he's a lot of fun to be with."

No one knew then that someday Trump would run for president. (When he does, he'll attack Hillary Clinton for Bill Clinton's own entanglements with Epstein.) But Trump's already ahead of the curve in that he ends up severing his ties to Epstein well before the police or the media get wind of Epstein's penchant for underage girls.

He does this because he finds out that in their endless hunt for "masseuses," Epstein's procurers have been prowling around Trump's estate in Palm Beach.

CHAPTER 33

Virginia Roberts: 1999

Trump's estate, Mar-a-Lago, had once belonged to the fabulously wealthy heiress Marjorie Merriweather Post. It sits on twenty perfectly manicured acres less than two miles away from Jeffrey Epstein's home on El Brillo Way. It's home to the exclusive Mar-a-Lago Club, which has a spa, tennis courts, and a very posh restaurant.

Donald Trump had fought the town council for decades as they blocked all his efforts to turn the place into a private resort. Other clubs on the island—those with a history of excluding blacks and Jews—had never faced such restrictions, Trump had argued. At one point he sent copies of two movies to every member of the town council: *Guess Who's Coming to Dinner,* in which Sidney Poitier confronts his girlfriend's racist parents, and *Gentleman's Agreement,* in which a journalist confronts anti-Semitism in Connecticut and New York City.

"Whether they love me or not, everyone agrees the greatest and most important place in Palm Beach is Mar-a-Lago," Trump told the *Washington Post* after winning his battle. "I took this ultimate place and made it incredible and opened it, essentially, to the people of Palm Beach. The fact that I owned it made it a lot easier to get along with the Palm Beach establishment."

The Breakers hotel, Trump explained, "gets the [island's] leftovers."

It cost $100,000 to join the club. Members paid $14,000 yearly in dues. And although Epstein had never properly joined the club, Trump's friendship with Ghislaine Maxwell gave Epstein unlimited use of the facilities.

This arrangement ended when a member's young daughter complained to her wealthy father: while relaxing at Mar-a-Lago, she'd been approached and invited out to Epstein's house.

The girl said that she had gone and that Epstein had tried to get her to undress.

The girl's father had gone directly to Trump, who—in no uncertain terms—told Epstein that he was barred from Mar-a-Lago.

Because no complaint was filed, the police had taken no action. But years later, a woman named Virginia Roberts would say that, as a young girl, she'd had an identical encounter at Mar-a-Lago.

According to a court document Virginia filed in her civil lawsuit against Epstein, she was a changing-room assistant at Mar-a-Lago, earning about nine dollars an hour, when Ghislaine Maxwell approached her. Maxwell asked Virginia if she was interested in learning to be a massage therapist—which, it turned out, she was. Like the other girl, Virginia told her father, who was also employed at Mar-a-Lago as a maintenance manager. But Virginia's father saw nothing wrong with the offer, and he drove her, later that day, to Epstein's house on El Brillo Way.

There, according to the document, Maxwell assured

Virginia's father that Ms. Maxwell would provide trans-
portation home for his teenage daughter. Then she led
Virginia upstairs, to a spa room equipped with a shower
and a massage table. Jeffrey Epstein was lying, naked, on
the table.

Virginia was shocked, she says in the filing, but, with
no experience with massages, thought this could be massage therapy protocol. "Ms. Maxwell then took off her
own shirt and left on her underwear and started rub-
bing her breasts across [Jeffrey's] body, impliedly showing [Virginia] what she was expected to do," the filing
continues. "Ms. Maxwell then told [Virginia] to take
off her clothes. The minor girl was apprehensive about
doing this, but, in fear, proceeded to follow Ms. Maxwell by removing everything but her underwear. She
was then ordered to remove her underwear and straddle
[Epstein]. The encounter escalated, with [Jeffrey] and
Ms. Maxwell sexually assaulting, battering, exploiting,
and abusing [Virginia] in various ways and in various
locations, including the steam room and the shower. At
the end of this sexually exploitive abuse, [Epstein] and
Ms. Maxwell giddily told [Virginia] to return the following day and told her she had 'lots of potential.' [Epstein]
paid [Virginia] hundreds of dollars, told her it was for
two hours of work, and directed one of her employees to
drive her home."

At the time, Virginia was fifteen years old.

CHAPTER 34

Declaration of Virginia Roberts Giuffre: January 19, 2015, filed on January 19, 2015 by attorneys representing Jeffrey Epstein's victims

1. *My name is Virginia Giuffre and I was born in August, 1983.*

2. *I am currently 31 years old.*

3. *I grew up in Palm Beach, Florida. When I was little, I loved animals and wanted to be a veterinarian. But my life took a very different turn when adults—including Jeffrey Epstein and his close friend Alan Dershowitz—began to be interested in having sex with me.*

4. *In approximately 1999, when I was 15 years old, I met Ghislaine Maxwell. She is the daughter of Robert Maxwell, who had been a wealthy publisher in Britain. Maxwell asked that I come with her to Jeffrey Epstein's mansion for the purposes of teaching me how to perform "massages" and to train me personally in that area. Soon after that I went to Epstein's home in Palm Beach on El Brillo Way.*

5. *From the first time I was taken to Epstein's mansion that day, his motivations and actions were sexual, as were Maxwell's. My father was not allowed inside. I was brought up some stairs. There was a naked guy, Epstein, on the table in the room. Epstein and Maxwell forced me into sexual activity with Epstein. I was 15 years old at the time. He seemed to be in his 40s or 50s. I was paid $200. I was driven home by one of Epstein's employees.*

6. *I came back for several days following and did the same sorts of sexual things for Epstein.*

7. *After I did those things for Epstein, he and Maxwell said they were going to have me travel and were going to get an education for me. They were promising me the world, that I would travel with Epstein on his private jet and have a well-paid profession. Epstein said he would eventually match me up with a wealthy person so that I would be "set up" for life.*

8. *So I started "working" exclusively for Epstein. He took me to New York on his big, private jet. We went to his mansion in New York City. I was shown to my room, a very luxurious room. The mansion was huge. I was very young and I got scared because it was so big. Epstein brought me to a room with a massage parlor. Epstein made me engage [in] sexual activities with him there.*

9. *You can see how young I looked in the photograph below [see insert page 3].*

10. *Epstein took me on a ferry boat on one of the trips to New York City and there he took the picture above. I was approximately 15 or 16 years old at the time.*

11. *Over the next few weeks, Jeffrey Epstein and Ghislaine Maxwell trained me to do what they*

wanted, including sexual activities. The training was in New York and Florida, at Epstein's mansion. It was basically every day and it was like going to school. I also had to have sex with Epstein many times.

12. I was trained to be "everything a man wanted me to be." It wasn't just sexual training—they wanted me to be able to cater to all the needs of the men they were going to send me to. They said that they loved that I was very compliant and knew how to keep my mouth shut about what they expected me to do.

13. Epstein and Maxwell also told me that they wanted me to produce information for them in addition to performing sex on the men. They told me to pay attention to the details about what the men wanted, so I could report back to them.

14. While I had juvenile hopes of bettering my life, from very early on I was also afraid of Epstein. Epstein told me he was a billionaire. I told my mother that I was working for this rich guy, and she said "go, go far away." Epstein had promised me a lot, and I knew if I left I would be in big trouble. I was witness to a lot of illegal and bad behavior by Epstein and his friends. If I left Epstein, he knew all kinds of powerful people. He could have had me killed or abducted, and I knew he was capable of that if I did not obey him. He let me know that he knew many people in high places. Speaking about himself, he said "I can get away" with things. Even as a teenager, I understood what this meant and it scared me, as I believe he intended.

15. I visited and traveled with Jeffrey Epstein from 1999 through the summer of 2002, and during that time I stayed with him for sexual activities at each of his houses (or mansions) in locations including New York City, New York; the area of Santa Fe, New

Mexico; Palm Beach, Florida; an island in the U.S. Virgin Islands; and Paris, France. I had sex with him often in these places and also with the various people he demanded that I have sex with. Epstein paid me for many of these sexual encounters. Looking back, I realize that my only purposes for Epstein, Maxwell, and their friends was to be used for sex.

16. To illustrate my connection to these places, I include four photographs taken of me in New Mexico [see insert page 3 for one of the photographs mentioned]. The first one is a museum in Santa Fe, New Mexico. We had gone sightseeing for the day. Epstein took this picture of me. I was approximately 17 at the time, judging from the looks of it. At the end of the day we returned to Epstein's Zorro Ranch. The second picture is me on one of Epstein's horses on the ranch in New Mexico. The following two are from wintertime in New Mexico.

17. When I was with him, Epstein had sex with underage girls on a daily basis. His interest in this kind of sex was obvious to the people around him. The activities were so obvious and bold that anyone spending any significant time at one of Epstein's residences would have clearly been aware of what was going on.

18. Epstein's code word for sexual encounters was that it was a "massage." At times the interaction between Epstein and the girls would start in the massage room setting, but it was always a sexual encounter and never just a massage.

19. In addition to constantly finding underage girls to satisfy their personal desires, Epstein and Maxwell also got girls for Epstein's friends and acquaintances. Epstein specifically told me that the reason for him doing this was so that they would "owe him," they would "be in his pocket," and he would "have

something on them." I understood that Epstein thought he could get leniency if he was ever caught doing anything illegal, or that he could escape trouble altogether.

Roberts submitted her declaration in support of a motion to be added as a plaintiff in a suit (ongoing, as of this writing) that sought to overturn a non-prosecution agreement that Jeffrey Epstein would reach with the government. Roberts was seeking to join a case brought against the government by two other victims, but a judge denied her motion in April of 2015, explaining that the case had already been pending for several years, and it was unneccesary to add an additional plaintiff.

Roberts's declaration, which goes on for another eight pages, and makes twenty-four additional points, was stricken from the record—the judge explained that the "lurid" and "unnecessary details" involving "non-parties" to the lawsuit against the government, were "immaterial and impertinent" to the proceedings.

Through a representative, Ghislaine Maxwell called the allegations against her "obvious lies," after which Roberts filed a defamation suit against Maxwell. In an answer filed in the suit, Maxwell elaborated that Roberts's "story of abuse at the hands of Ms. Maxwell" was "fabricated" for financial gain.

CHAPTER 35

Alicia: May 20, 1997

Donald Trump's instincts regarding Jeffrey Epstein were solid. But if the reporters who were beginning to look into Epstein's mysterious background had dug a bit further, there's a chance they would have hit pay dirt as well—and not just in Palm Beach.

In California, for instance, a paper trail already stretched from the Santa Monica Police Department to Epstein's front door.

In the spring—almost the summer—of 1997, a call came in to the police. The young woman who placed it—a young actress who'd appeared on *Baywatch* and *General Hospital*—said she'd been sexually assaulted at a trendy hotel called Shutters on the Beach.

The officer who took the call knew the woman's name—Alicia*—and her voice. A week earlier, she'd told him about an encounter with Epstein. The woman had not wanted to make a formal complaint at the time.

---

* Alicia's name, some identifying details, and dialogue have been changed.

But she had taken the cop's card, and now he was happy to hear that she'd changed her mind.

In a shaky voice, Alicia described Epstein as a tall-ish man—five feet eleven or six feet in height was her guess—with gray hair and brown eyes. He was the owner of a large black four-door Mercedes and was a regular at Shutters on the Beach, which was the kind of place that cost one thousand dollars a night and was frequented by actors, agents, and other Hollywood types.

Alicia told the cop that she was a model and actress herself. She'd known Epstein for about a month. They had a friend in common, and she'd sent him her head shots.

Then, through an assistant, Epstein had invited her to meet in his room at the hotel.

Alicia said she was having reservations, the officer wrote in his report, *because generally interviews are not conducted in hotel rooms.*

According to her, things turned frightening quickly.

> *She was unsure she was safe because although she wanted to land the job as a 'Victoria's Secret' catalog model she felt as though Epstein was attempting to get her to act in an unprofessional manner for a model.*

Epstein wore navy blue sweatpants and a white T-shirt, she recalled. The T-shirt had the letters *USA* printed on it in patriotic red, white, and blue.

> *Epstein told her to undress and actually assisted her to do so while saying 'let me manhandle you for a second.'*

Then, Alicia told the cop, *Epstein groped her buttocks against her will while acting as though he was evaluating her body*. Alicia had stopped Epstein, and left the room, but couldn't get over the incident.

At the top of his crime report, the officer wrote "Sexual Battery." But Epstein was never charged in the incident. "The Santa Monica Police Department discounted every one of [Alicia's] allegations of improper conduct by Jeffrey Epstein and they took no action on this 1997 complaint," Epstein's West Palm Beach attorney, Jack Goldberger, told the *Palm Beach Post* in 2010.

"The cops said it'd be my word against his," Alicia told the paper. "And since he had a lot of money, I let it go. I hadn't thought much about it since, until I saw his picture online. And now, I want everybody to know how much of a creep he's always been."

CHAPTER 36

Graydon Carter: December 2002

G raydon Carter, the legendary editor of *Vanity Fair,* likes to get to his office early, well before the rest of his staff files in.

Most monthly magazines operate at a leisurely pace—three weeks of coming up with ideas, assigning articles, and shooting the shit in the corporate kitchen followed by one frantic week when all the actual editing gets done. But this isn't the case at *Vanity Fair,* which runs hard-hitting investigative pieces alongside its glitzy celebrity profiles. There are also parties to plan and host—incredibly glamorous parties, including the annual Oscar-night bash, which is more fun and far more exclusive than the Academy Awards ceremony itself. *Vanity Fair* is an old, famous brand. But Carter is its public face, just as Anna Wintour is the face of Condé Nast's iconic fashion magazine, *Vogue.*

One cover of *Vanity Fair* can turn a minor celebrity into a superstar. And a single thoroughly researched story can bring down a corporate overlord.

Carter's easy to recognize: the pompadour of white

hair, like a lion's mane. The Santa Claus body stuffed into an impeccably tailored bespoke suit. He wears his fame lightly. But he could not be more serious about his responsibilities, which are weighing heavily on him this month. Months earlier, he'd assigned a piece to Vicky Ward, an Englishwoman who wrote frequently for *Vanity Fair*. He'd meant for it to be an easy assignment: Ward was pregnant with twins. She wasn't allowed to fly. But here was a story right on her doorstep. A nice, easy profile of Jeffrey Epstein. Who was he, really? Carter knew he threw fabulous parties attended by academics, billionaires, and beautiful women. Recently he'd flown Bill Clinton to Africa. But no one seemed to know how he had made his fortune. Epstein's story reminded the editor of F. Scott Fitzgerald's *The Great Gatsby*.

Carter himself could have stepped out of a novel—though in his case, the author would be Horatio Alger. A Canadian college dropout who'd worked as a railroad lineman, he arrived in New York in his late twenties and commenced an astonishingly quick rise up the social and media ladders. But where Carter was open and outgoing, Epstein really was Gatsby-like—very little about him was known. Maybe, Carter thought, Ward could find out. What did Epstein do, exactly, for money? Why was he so secretive? Why were so many brilliant and powerful men drawn to him? And where did those beautiful women come from?

Almost immediately, Epstein began a campaign to discredit Ward. He prevailed upon Conrad Black, the press baron and Epstein's Palm Beach neighbor—who was also a step-uncle of Vicky Ward's husband—to ask Ward to drop the story. But Ward was tenacious, and what she came back with was dynamite. More interesting and much more salacious than anything Carter had imagined.

Now Carter's staff was putting in the hours it would take to confirm all the things she'd uncovered, picking the ones they could publish and laying them all out in a narrative that would be no less explosive than the facts it contained.

CHAPTER 37

Vicky Ward: October 2002

Epstein went out of his way to spin the *Vanity Fair* story to his own ends, and soon after she got the assignment, Vicky Ward's phone began to ring off the hook: calls from Ace Greenberg and Jimmy Cayne, the current head of Bear Stearns; from Les Wexner; from academics, scientists, and movers and shakers who counted Epstein among their friends.

Then there were the calls from Epstein himself. He wouldn't go on the record, but despite the rumors he'd spread behind Ward's back, he was happy to talk informally, even give her a tour of his Manhattan mansion and trot out stories that he had dined out on for years. By most accounts, Epstein could be extremely charming— even if it had taken Ghislaine to teach him which forks to use when—and he did his best to charm Vicky Ward. But she was not easily seduced, and she turned out to have a keen eye for Epstein's missteps.

Over tea in his town house, she noticed, Epstein ate all the finger food that had been put out for both of them. She found it odd that the only book this supposedly brilliant man had left for her to see was a paperback by the Marquis de Sade. And then there was the call afterward from one of Epstein's assistants—a woman Ward did not know—who told her, "Jeffrey wanted me to tell you that you looked so pretty."

Ward *is* pretty, with fine English features and flowing blond hair. She was also *very* pregnant then, with a bad case of morning sickness. She threw up often, sometimes in public, and these clumsy advances on Epstein's part only added to her ever-present nausea. For a man who was supposedly brilliant, he'd struck her, oddly, as not very *smart*.

"Epstein is charming, but he doesn't let the charm slip into his eyes," she wrote. "They are steely and calculating, giving some hint at the steady whir of machinery running behind them. 'Let's play chess,' he said to me, after refusing to give an interview for this article. 'You be white. You get the first move.' It was an appropriate metaphor for a man who seems to feel he can win no matter what the advantage of the other side. *His* advantage is that no one really seems to know him or his history completely or what his arsenal actually consists of. He has carefully engineered it so that he remains one of the few truly baffling mysteries among New York's moneyed world. People know snippets, but few know the whole."

The testimonials Epstein's friends gave were glowing: "I think we both possess the skill of seeing patterns," Les Wexner told her. "Jeffrey sees patterns in politics and financial markets, and I see patterns in lifestyle and fashion trends. My skills are not in investment strategy, and, as everyone who knows Jeffrey knows, his are not in fashion and design. We frequently discuss world trends as each of us sees them."

"I'm on my 20th book," said Alan Dershowitz, who'd

met Epstein in 1997. "The only person outside of my immediate family that I send drafts to is Jeffrey."

But Ward also talked to other sources, who had their own questions and qualms about Jeffrey Epstein. Some were involved in lawsuits against him. Others had served on prestigious boards with him. One who had witnessed Epstein's aborted stint on the board of Rockefeller University called him arrogant.

One powerful investment manager wondered about Epstein's conspicuous absence from New York's trading floors. "The trading desks don't seem to know him," he says. "It's unusual for animals *that* big to not leave any footprints in the snow."

Ward uncovered legal documents, including Epstein's interview with the SEC, given in the wake of his departure from Bear Stearns. She visited a federal prison in Massachusetts and spoke at length with Steven Hoffenberg, who told her that Epstein had made a major mistake in taking Bill Clinton to Africa. "I always told him to stay below the radar," Hoffenberg said. He made other accusations, about Epstein's financial practices, which Epstein denied—and Ward knew that Hoffenberg, the Ponzi-scheme mastermind, was not to be trusted. But she did find it strange that throughout the reporting process Epstein was much less openly concerned with what she'd found out about his finances than with what she'd uncovered about his dealings with women.

Time and again, he would call and ask her: "What do you have on the *girls?*"

One young woman Ward talked to had been invited by Ghislaine Maxwell to attend a party at Epstein's town house. There, the woman had noticed, female guests far outnumbered the male guests. "These were not women you'd see at Upper East Side dinners," the woman had said. "Many seemed foreign and dressed a little bizarrely."

"This same guest also attended a cocktail party thrown by Maxwell that Prince Andrew attended, which was filled, she says, with young Russian models," Ward wrote. "'Some of the guests were horrified,' the woman says."

Another source, one who had worked with Epstein, said, "He's reckless, and he's gotten more so. Money does that to you. He's breaking the oath he made to himself— that he would never do anything that would expose him in the media. Right now, in the wake of the publicity following his trip with Clinton, he must be in a very difficult place."

CHAPTER 38

Vicky Ward: November 2002

W hat I had 'on the girls,'" Ward explained in a *Daily Beast* article published after Epstein's arrest, "were some remarkably brave first-person accounts. Three on-the-record stories from a family: a mother and her daughters who came from Phoenix. The oldest daughter, an artist whose character was vouchsafed to me by several sources, including the artist Eric Fischl, had told me, weeping as she sat in my living room, of how Epstein had attempted to seduce both her and, separately, her younger sister, then only 16."

Ward had written it all down in her notes. She had crossed the t's, dotted the i's.

But when she called Epstein to get his response, he denied the allegations completely.

"Just the mention of a 16-year-old girl," Epstein told her, "carries the wrong impression. I don't see what it adds to the piece. And that makes me unhappy."

If some sort of criminal investigation had taken place, that would have been one thing. But, at that time, no criminal investigation into Epstein's affairs had been launched. And in the absence of an investigation, the rumors of Epstein's dealings with very young women seemed to be just that—rumors.

Graydon Carter consulted his lawyers, his editors, and his fact-checkers. And then something odd and disturbing happened at the Condé Nast building, then in Times Square.

As usual, Carter had come into the office early. He swiped his key card in the lobby, pressed the elevator button, and arrived in the hallway outside the reception area on the twenty-first floor.

It would have been a perfect time to review Ward's story.

Her description of Epstein's town house—which is said to have been the largest private residence in New York City at the time—was priceless: "Inside, amid the flurry of menservants attired in sober black suits and pristine white gloves, you feel you have stumbled into someone's private Xanadu," she'd written. "This is no mere rich person's home, but a high-walled, eclectic, imperious fantasy that seems to have no boundaries. The entrance hall is decorated not with paintings but with row upon row of individually framed eyeballs; these, the owner tells people with relish, were imported from England, where they were made for injured soldiers. Next comes a marble foyer, which does have a painting, in the manner of Jean Dubuffet...but the host coyly refuses to tell visitors who painted it. In any case, guests are like pygmies next to the nearby twice-life-size sculpture of a naked African warrior."

The journalist had confirmed that several prominent names—Mort Zuckerman, the famous real estate mogul and publisher; Microsoft executive Nathan Myhrvold;

and Donald Trump among them—had dined at the residence. She'd interviewed several of Epstein's friends and ex-friends: Nobel Prize–winning scientists, financiers who worked with Epstein at Bear Stearns. She'd handled Steven Hoffenberg with aplomb. And, working with *Vanity Fair*'s editors, she'd figured out ways to slip even more information between the lines, in ways that would allow readers to form their own questions about Epstein's finances.

In that respect, she'd fulfilled her original assignment perfectly.

What Carter needed to figure out was what to do with the artist, her sister, and their mother's story. But before he could swipe his key card to let himself into the magazine's offices, Carter saw a man standing in the reception area.

The man was motionless. He'd been waiting for Carter.

It was Jeffrey Epstein. Nonplussed, Carter invited him into his office.

Epstein denied the claims involving underage women. No criminal charges had been filed. And so *Vanity Fair* decided not to include the claims in Ward's article. But, according to Ward, when her editor Doug Stumpf called her, she cried.

She'd worked so hard on the piece, gotten so stressed out that one of her twins had begun to grow more slowly than the other. On doctor's orders, she'd been put on bed rest.

"Why?" she asked when she got to speak to Carter directly.

"He's sensitive about the young women. And we still get to run most of the piece."

In her notebook, Ward wrote down the rest of what Carter had said: "I believe him," he told her. "I'm Canadian."

But the piece that came out, in the March issue, still created a sensation. It was called "The Talented Mr. Epstein" in a sly reference to Patricia Highsmith's celebrated suspense novel *The Talented Mr. Ripley*. The film adaptation, by Anthony Minghella, was still fresh in the minds of *Vanity Fair*'s readers. For Graydon Carter, just posing the question *Is Epstein some sort of scam artist, like Ripley?* had been question enough. And throughout the piece, there were ironies readers wouldn't miss as they drew their own conclusions about Epstein's life story. It came through clearly in the first line of the last paragraph of Ward's 7,500-word story: "Many people comment there is something innocent, almost childlike about Jeffrey Epstein."

In context, the word *innocent* was rather ironic—so much so that it almost became its own opposite.

CHAPTER 39

Todd Meister: June 2015

Harry Cipriani, on Fifth Avenue, is a New York institution. The restaurant began its life as an American outpost of Harry's Bar—which was itself a famous American outpost in Venice. Located inside the Sherry-Netherland hotel, it's a theme restaurant—the theme being money. And today, a hedge-fund manager named Todd Meister is talking about a very wealthy man—Jeffrey Epstein—whom he knows through his father, Epstein's sometime friend Bob Meister.

"I've known Jeffrey since I was nineteen," Meister says. "So let me tell you what I know—whatever everyone knows and everybody else says. First off, he's no billionaire. Second off—and here's why—he has no clue how to invest. He has people do that for him."

Meister knows how to invest. He does it for other people and, as the son of a superrich father, for himself. He also knows about the good life. Parties in Vegas; weekends in the Hamptons; affairs with beautiful women that end up getting splashed all over the tabloids.

It makes sense that, once upon a time, he and Epstein would have gotten along.

"As for the girls," Meister says, "that was just business. He'd seat them strategically at client dinners. When he went to the movies, he'd take three or four girls with him. They'd take turns massaging his back, arms, and legs."

According to Meister, Epstein used to boast that he "liked to go into insane asylums because he liked to fuck crazy women."

"Who knows if it's true?" Meister adds. "But I'm telling you, he used to say it."

From time to time, Epstein's friends and acquaintances would see sides of Epstein that he'd grown much less shy about sharing.

Epstein encouraged Alan Dershowitz to invest with a prominent hedge-fund manager named Orin Kramer. Dershowitz did, and he made a lot of money at first. But in 2008, the fund Dershowitz had invested in lost a substantial amount. Afterward, according to a former associate of Epstein's, Epstein appeared in Kramer's midtown Manhattan office. There, sources say, he told Kramer: "It's very much in your interest to make Alan Dershowitz whole."

Epstein's intervention worked, and Dershowitz recovered his money.

To people who'd known Epstein back in the 1980s, this kind of behavior was out of character. But the thing about Epstein was that you never could figure him out. One minute he was charming. The most charming man you'd ever meet. The next he was snarl, threat, and bluster. Something didn't add up. So you'd run the numbers: this many parties, that many women. Even with the connection to Victoria's Secret, the women didn't add up, either.

Throw in the modeling agency, it makes more sense. Then you plug in the parties. The scene brings *Eyes Wide Shut* to mind. But the thing is, *Eyes Wide Shut* only works in the shadows. For Epstein, getting on that plane with Clinton was more like a moment in *Caddyshack*—the one in which the groundhog peeks out from his hole in the golf course. From there on in, Jeffrey Epstein was like the mole in a game of whack-a-mole. It was only a matter of time before he'd be caught. But the question you had to ask yourself was, are people like Epstein born without morals? Or are their morals like snakeskin—just something they shed (along with all the other basic, day-to-day concerns that everyday working people have) as they make their way into that *Eyes Wide Shut* world?

Todd Meister, who was married to Nicky Hilton and stole the heiress Samantha Boardman away from Condé Nast's former editorial director James Truman, should know. He wonders out loud:

"How *does* a yutz like Epstein get beautiful women?"

At Harry Cipriani, the question lingers in the air.

PART IV

The Investigation

CHAPTER 40

Michael Reiter: January 2006

As far as Michael Reiter's concerned, the case that his team has built against Epstein—slowly, meticulously, over the course of an entire year—is airtight. Even now, Detective Recarey's finding new pieces of evidence. And already Reiter's been laying the groundwork with prosecutors. State attorney Barry Krischer has a reputation for toughness. He's known, nationally, for his prosecution of juvenile offenders. And Reiter's been keeping him abreast of the investigation. With Jeffrey Epstein, it's not simply a matter of seeing him punished. It's a matter of getting a sexual predator off the streets of Palm Beach.

Krischer assures the chief that he's taking this case *very* seriously.

The state attorney's office will have Reiter's back at every turn.

"I told him that we had an investigation that was very serious that involved a very noteworthy person and that involved a number of underage females," Reiter would say in his deposition for the suit that was later settled by

Epstein. "That it was of a sexual nature. I was concerned that we had not reached all of the victims, and we hadn't, I'm sure, at this point. I told him that I felt like the suspect would probably become aware of the investigation at some point and that we should probably expect some contact from…Mr. Epstein's lawyers. And I told him that I wanted to keep him very well informed on this and that I hoped that he would do the same. And that we would have to have more contact in making sure it was handled responsibly, intelligently, and appropriately as it moved forward."

Reiter would say that Epstein's name did not seem to ring a bell with the state attorney. But shortly afterward, the chief became aware that in certain powerful circles his investigation was being looked upon unfavorably. "I had many people-related conversations…on the cocktail-party circuit that suggested we approach this in a way that wasn't necessary," he would say.

Michael Reiter was a good cop. A good man. But he was about to discover that when it came to men with the power and influence Epstein wielded, fairness under the law was a relative, malleable concept.

CHAPTER 41

Detective Recarey: February 2006

For months, Joe Recarey's been interviewing girls who'd been brought to Epstein's house, subpoenaing telephone and car-rental records, conducting surveillance. Ultimately, according to a source within the Palm Beach PD, the department would identify forty-seven underage girls who'd been molested on El Brillo Way.

Recarey interviewed one of Epstein's pilots, a man named David Rogers, as well as Epstein's houseman, Alfredo Rodriguez. He also spoke to a woman who really *was* a massage therapist.

It turned out that Epstein paid just one hundred dollars for actual Swedish deep-tissue massages that the therapist provided for him and his friends, the lawyer Alan Dershowitz among them.

Did anything untoward ever happen? Recarey asked. Had Epstein ever asked the woman to rub his chest?

No, she told him. She wasn't Epstein's type. The girls she'd seen at his house were very thin and beautiful and did not have tattoos. This massage therapist had several tattoos that were visible, and on quite a few occasions Epstein and Ghislaine Maxwell had made negative comments about them.

According to a Palm Beach Police Department Incident Report filed by Recarey on July 25, 2006, the detective had also heard from Mary's father, who said that a private eye had been to his house, photographing his family and chasing visitors away.

Mary's dad had gotten the license plate—Florida E79-4EG.

Recarey traced it back to one Ivan Robles of West Palm Beach. Robles turned out to be a licensed private investigator.

Recarey informed the state's attorney's office.

Alison also contacted Recarey and told him that she'd been approached by someone who was in touch with Epstein. Alison had been told that she'd receive money if she would refuse to cooperate with the police.

Those who help him will be compensated, she was told, according to Detective Recarey's incident report. "And those who hurt him will be dealt with."

Recarey reassured the girl and told her that tampering with a witness in a case like this was a serious, arrestable offense.

Then he told an assistant state attorney.

The detective was leaving no *i* undotted and no *t* uncrossed.

But he did wonder if the state attorney's office itself had become part of the problem.

Epstein's Palm Beach property, 358 El Brillo Way (© *Chris Bott / Splash News / Corbis*)

One of the photographs captured on video during the Palm Beach Police Department search warrant walk-through of Epstein's El Brillo Way residence (*Palm Beach Police Department*)

Jeffrey Epstein's 1969 high school yearbook photo (*Lafayette High School, Brooklyn, New York, 1969*)

Jeffrey Epstein, Coney Island, circa 1969 (*Anonymous*)

(L to R) Jeffrey Epstein, Ghislaine Maxwell, and Tony Randall, who presided over a November 1991 YIVO Institute event at the Plaza Hotel to honor the late Robert Maxwell (*Marina Garnier*)

(L to R) Deborah Blohm, Jeffrey Epstein, Ghislaine Maxwell, and Gwendolyn Beck attend a reception at Mar-a-Lago, 1995 (*Davidoff Studios*)

Jeffrey Epstein, Donald Trump, and (newly signed Trump Model) Ingrid Seynhaeve attending the Victoria's Secret Angels party at Laura Belle club in New York City on April 8, 1997 (*Marina Garnier*)

Virginia Roberts, age fifteen; photo reportedly taken by Jeffrey Epstein in New York City (*Virginia Roberts Affidavit, US District Southern Court of Florida*)

(L to R) Prince Andrew, Virginia Roberts, and Ghislaine Maxwell; photo reportedly taken by Epstein with Roberts's camera in Maxwell's London town house. Roberts was seventeen years old at this time. (*Virginia Roberts Affidavit, US District Southern Court of Florida*)

Virginia Roberts, age seventeen; photo reportedly taken by Jeffrey Epstein at Zorro Ranch, his New Mexico property, in winter (*Virginia Roberts Affidavit, US District Southern Court of Florida*)

Jeffrey Epstein with Professor Alan Dershowitz in Cambridge, MA, September 8, 2004 (*© Rick Friedman / Corbis*)

On the day the police investigation began, Epstein was photographed with Ghislaine Maxwell in New York City at the 2005 Wall Street concert series benefiting Wall Street Rising, at Cipriani, March 15, 2005. *(Joe Shildhorn / Patrick McMullen)*

Jeffrey Epstein, photographed with Adrianna Ross, attending the launch of *Radar* magazine held at the Hotel QT in New York City, May 2005 *(Neil Rasmus / PatrickMcMullan.com / Sipa Press)*

2008 Palm Beach County Sheriff's Office booking photo of Jeffrey Epstein *(Palm Beach County Sheriff's Office)*

The Stockade, where Epstein served his sentence, photographed here in 2006, is located at 673 Fairgrounds Road in West Palm Beach, Florida. At the time, it was used as a minimum- and medium-security facility housing women and juveniles, as well as male inmates on a work-release program. *(Smith Aerial Photos)*

Epstein pleaded guilty to state solicitation charges and served thirteen months of an eighteen-month sentence, with liberal work-release privileges, in a solitary cell at the Palm Beach County Stockade similar to the one pictured here. (*Courtesy CDC Special Management, Palm Beach Sheriff's Office*)

Epstein and lawyer at the West Palm Beach courthouse in June 2008 to enter a plea nearly two years after being charged (*Uma Sanghvi / The Palm Beach Post / ZUMAPRESS.com*)

Jeffrey Epstein's entry in the National Sex Offender Registry (*National Sex Offender Registry*)

Epstein's Little Saint James island, US Virgin Islands: a privately owned cay (nicknamed Little Saint Jeff's) whose owner locals affectionately refer to as Richie Rich (© *Chris Bott / Splash News / Corbis*)

Epstein's Gulfstream, photographed on Little Saint James island in the US Virgin Islands, January 2015 (© *Chris Bott / Splash News / Corbis*)

Epstein's longtime pilot, Larry Visoski, was at the controls as Epstein's Gulfstream left Teterboro Airport in New Jersey, January 2016. (*Jae Donnelly*)

When Prince Andrew and Epstein were seen strolling together through New York's Central Park in 2011, shortly after Epstein's release from jail, the duke was forced to quit his role as the British government's global trade envoy. (*Jae Donnelly / News of the World*)

Stephen Hawking, photographed in March 2006 aboard an Atlantis submarine that was custom-fitted by Epstein to accommodate his wheelchair. Hawking was attending the conference "Confronting Gravity," "a workshop to explore fundamental questions in physics and cosmology," sponsored by the J. Epstein VI Foundation and the Center for Education and Research in Cosmology and Astrophysics (CERCA) at Case Western Reserve University, at the Ritz-Carlton, St. Thomas, USVI. (*Courtesy CERCA, Case Western University*)

A framed photo of Florida governor Charlie Crist and Scott Rothstein in Rothstein's office in Fort Lauderdale, autographed by Charlie Crist. *Scott—You are amazing! Charlie Crist (Carline Jean © Sun Sentinel / ZUMAPRESS.com)*

Epstein's current residence, the storied building formerly known as the Herbert N. Straus Mansion, on East 71st Street just off Central Park, was acquired by Leslie Wexner in 1989. *(Laura Hanifin)*

Epstein, a longtime benefactor, with an unidentified friend, attended the 2014 New York Academy of Art's Tribeca Ball, presented by Van Cleef & Arpels, at the New York Academy of Art on April 7, 2014, in New York City. *(Billy Farrell / BFAnyc.com)*

Nadia Marcinkova, Michele Tagliani, Sarah Kellen, and Teala Davies, photographed at the New York Academy of Art's Tribeca Ball, April 14, 2004 *(Rob Rich / SocietyAllure.com)*

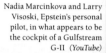

Sarah (formerly Kellen/Kensington) and husband, NASCAR driver Brian Vickers, arrive on the red carpet at the 141st running of the Kentucky Derby at Churchill Downs in Louisville, Kentucky *(Jeff Moreland / Icon Sportswire via AP Images)*

Nadia Marcinkova and Larry Visoski, Epstein's personal pilot, in what appears to be the cockpit of a Gulfstream G-II *(YouTube)*

Michael and Janet Reiter at the Palm Beach Police Foundation Policemen's Ball at Mar-a-Lago, January 2012 *(Debbie Schatz / Palm Beach Daily News / ZUMAPRESS.com)*

Retired Palm Beach police detective Joe Recarey, November 2013 *(Meghan McCarthy / Palm Beach Daily News / ZUMAPRESS.com)*

Police nationale ✓
@PoliceNationale

[#AppelàTémoins] La #police judiciaire, sous la direction du Parquet de Paris, recherche des témoins dans l'affaire #Epstein.
Des policiers spécialisés sont mobilisés.

Si vous avez été victime ou témoin, contactez:
📞 06 83 67 43 57
📧 temoignage-ocrvp@interieur.gouv.fr

The French National Police's Twitter calls for witnesses in the Epstein case to come forward. (© *AP/Shutterstock*)

Geoffrey Berman, US attorney for the Southern District of New York, addressing the press on the new charges against Jeffrey Epstein, July 8, 2019 (© *Bloomberg/Getty Images*)

The Palm Beach, Florida, residence of Jeffrey Epstein (© *Wilfredo Lee/AP/Shutterstock*)

Following his conviction in 2008, Jeffrey Epstein registered at the Florida state office for sexual offenders. (© *Miami Herald/Getty Images*)

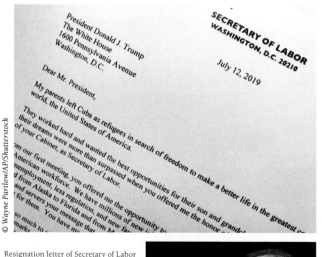

President Donald J. Trump
The White House
1600 Pennsylvania Avenue
Washington, D.C.

SECRETARY OF LABOR
WASHINGTON, D.C. 20210

July 12, 2019

Dear Mr. President,

My parents left Cuba as refugees in search of freedom to make a better life in the greatest of world, the United States of America.

They worked hard and wanted the best opportunities for their son and grand their dreams were more than surpassed when you offered me the honor of your Cabinet, as Secretary of Labor.

om our first meeting, you offered me the opportunity to American workforce. We have millions of new j employment, less regulation, and new far d from Alaska to Florida and from M and servers your message that for them. You have me so much to marks

Resignation letter of Secretary of Labor Alex Acosta, dated July 12, 2019. As the head of the US Attorney's Office in Miami, Florida, Acosta had handled a secret plea deal for Jeffrey Epstein, which resulted in his receiving a lenient sentence on state prostitution charges.

Courtroom sketch of New York federal court, Judge Richard Berman presiding. Jeffrey Epstein and attorney Martin Weinberg attend the bail hearing seeking Epstein's house arrest pending trial. Request denied. (© *Elizabeth Williams/AP/Shutterstock*)

The front door to Jeffrey Epstein's mansion on the Upper East Side of Manhattan, with his initials visible, inset into the wall on the left. The door was forcibly opened by investigators following his arrest. (© *JASON SZENES/EPA-EFE/Shutterstock*)

Michelle Licata, thirty, weeps at the recollection of sexual encounters with Jeffrey Epstein when she was sixteen. (© *Miami Herald/Getty Images*)

The notebook Michelle Licata kept as a teenager (© *Miami Herald/Getty Images*)

Virginia Roberts holds a photo of herself at age sixteen, the age she was when she says she was first abused by Epstein. (© *Miami Herald/Getty Images*)

Ghislaine Maxwell and Naomi Campbell at the Tribeca Film Festival, 2002. In August 2019, Campbell (right) posted a YouTube video addressing her ties with Epstein, calling his actions indefensible. (© *Mark Mainz/Getty Images*)

Protest group "Hot Mess" demonstrating in front of the federal courthouse in New York City on the day of Epstein's arrest (© *Stephanie Keith/Getty Images*)

Lawyer David Boies and alleged victim Annie Farmer depart Epstein's detention hearing, July 15, 2019 (© *TIMOTHY A. CLARY/ Getty Images*)

Courtroom artist's sketch of accusers Annie Farmer (at microphone) and Courtney Wild (far right) at Epstein's bail hearing in New York.. They were abused by the defendant, they said, from the ages of sixteen and fourteen, respectively. (© *Elizabeth Williams/ AP/Shutterstock*)

A 2017 photo of Jeffrey Epstein registered to the New York State Division of Criminal Justice Services list of sexual offenders (© *AP/Shutterstock*)

Officers patrol the Manhattan courthouse while Epstein is formally charged with sex trafficking, July 18, 2019 (© *Spencer Platt/Getty Images*)

By September 2019, billionaire Les Wexner, chairman and CEO of Victoria's Secret's parent company, publicly apologized for his ties to Epstein. (© *Jay LaPrete/ AP/Shutterstock*)

Joichi Ito resigned as director of the MIT Media Lab in September 2019 over revelations that his personal and professional ties to Epstein were far deeper than Ito had originally disclosed. (© *Phillip Faraone/Getty Images*)

Epstein began his career as a math and science teacher, and he used the riches he amassed to cultivate ties to leading influencers in those fields, as well as politics, culture, and the arts. (© *Rick Friedman/Getty Images*)

Following Jeffrey Epstein's death, the whereabouts of his longtime associate Ghislaine Maxwell have become the subject of intense scrutiny by law enforcement and the media. (© *Mathieu Polak/Getty Images*)

A photograph of Maxwell at a Los Angeles–area In-N-Out Burger restaurant made headlines in August 2019, but her whereabouts remain unknown.

Jeffrey Epstein's brother, Mark, with Polina Proshinka, New York Fashion Week, 2013. Mark Epstein was to inherit his brother's fortune—until Epstein changed his will two days before he died, instead leaving his vast wealth to "The 1953 Trust." (© *Patrick McMullan/Getty Images*)

Jeffrey Epstein had an apartment in this building in Paris, France, on Avenue Foch, near the Arc de Triomphe. Epstein's 8,600-square-foot luxury apartment, valued at $8.6 million, was raided by French police on September 23, 2019. (*Tim Malloy*)

CHAPTER 42

Barry Krischer: April 2006

State attorney Barry Krischer was an elected official, but before taking his post, he'd been a lawyer in private practice in and around Palm Beach. Elected twice to his office, in 1992 and 1996, he had run unopposed for state attorney in 2000 and 2004. During the course of his long career, which began in 1970 with a three-year stint in the district attorney's office in Brooklyn, he received a number of awards: the pro bono award from the Legal Aid Society of Palm Beach County for his service with the juvenile justice system and for his work with the child protection team; the Peace at Home award, presented by Governor Jeb Bush, for his work with victims of family violence; a lifetime achievement award from the Florida Bar. He was a board member of the National District Attorneys Association. And he was not necessarily averse to going after the rich and powerful. In 2003, he launched an investigation into Rush Limbaugh's use of, and means of obtaining, oxycodone and hydrocodone. (A few years after Limbaugh's arrest, which coincided with Chief Reiter's investigation into Jeffrey Epstein, the talk-show host settled with prosecutors, agreed to submit to random drug testing, and gave up his firearms permit.)

Krischer himself, however, had been accused of sexual misconduct.

In October of 1992, Jodi Bergeron, a legal secretary who'd worked for Krischer, filed a sexual harassment lawsuit against him in the Palm Beach County circuit court. That suit was dismissed, but a few months later, the woman took Krischer to federal court, accusing him of making unwanted advances and demanding recompense for battery, negligence, invasion of privacy, and emotional distress.

Krischer had placed his hands, violently, inside her blouse, the woman said. He'd forcibly fondled her breasts, forcibly kissed her, and rubbed her shoulders while brushing her buttocks with his hands and knees, all while accompanying the gestures with verbal advances.

When she declined those advances, the woman claimed, Krischer fired her.

Krischer denied the allegations. At the time, he was making his first run for the state attorney's office. The charges were politically motivated, he said. Members of a local chapter of NOW—the National Organization for Women—had stood by the lawyer, citing his efforts to stop domestic violence, among his other virtues.

"I am here to support Barry Krischer for the work his office did in my daughter's case," one woman said during a rally that took place in front of the courthouse. "Her murderer received the maximum sentence, a life sentence."

The second lawsuit had also been dismissed—after Krischer's former law firm agreed to pay Bergeron's attorney seven thousand dollars in legal fees.

* * *

Now Chief Reiter and Detective Recarey were beginning to have their own questions about Barry Krischer.
The Palm Beach PD wanted to charge Epstein with one
count of lewd and lascivious behavior and four counts of
unlawful sexual activity with a minor—felony charges
that would have amounted to years behind bars in the
case of a conviction. Wendy Dobbs and Sarah Kellen
would be charged as accomplices.

This was not the plan that Krischer seemed to have in
mind for Jeffrey Epstein.

In cases involving the sexual abuse of minors, prosecuting attorneys tend to have suspects arrested, then
push for a trial. But instead of granting his approval for
an arrest, Krischer told the police that he would convene
a grand jury, which would be asked to consider a broad
range of charges.

In a case such as Epstein's, this was highly unusual.
Not damning in and of itself. But very strange. In Florida, grand juries are only *required* in capital cases. At
the state attorney's discretion, they may also be called in
controversial cases—for instance, cases involving crimes
committed by public officials. But Jeffrey Epstein wasn't
a public official, and as far as the Palm Beach PD was
concerned, the only controversial thing about the case
they'd built was that Epstein was rich and well connected. In his deposition for *B.B. vs. Epstein,* Chief Reiter
relayed Krischer's concerns: the prosecutor had to make
sure that his case was solid, beyond a reasonable doubt.
And Krischer did have his doubts about the credibility
of the young women who'd be called to testify against
Epstein.

Even so, Reiter was beginning to wonder if Krischer
was stacking the deck in Epstein's favor—if, thanks to

the sway prosecutors have over grand juries, assembling such a jury wasn't an excellent way to let Epstein off with the lightest punishment possible.

Another unusual thing: the way Barry Krischer and the lawyers working for him ignored Chief Reiter's multiple phone calls as well as Detective Recarey's—even though the police had been hearing from Epstein's own lawyers.

"[Krischer] and I had an excellent relationship," Chief Reiter said in his deposition. "I was the speaker at his swearing-in ceremony. And that he wouldn't return my phone calls—I mean, it was clear to me by his actions that he could not objectively look at this case."

In the incident report he ended up writing, Detective Recarey remembered a phone call that he received from Guy Fronstin, one of the lawyers representing Epstein.

It was a message Epstein wanted to send, something central to the case that demanded explanation. The whole shit show swirling around him was just a misunderstanding—a misrepresentation—of Epstein's actual interests and intentions.

Fronstin says Mr. Epstein is very passionate about massages, Detective Recarey would write.

And: *Mr. Epstein had donated over $100,000 to the Ballet of Florida for massages.*

And: *The massages are therapeutic and spiritually sound for him. That is why he has had so many massages.*

CHAPTER 43

Palm Beach Police Department Incident Report Filed by Detective Joseph Recarey: July 25, 2006

On April 13 and April 14, 2006, I attempted contact on several occasions with ASA [assistant state attorney Daliah] Weiss and ASA [Lanna] Belohlavek to ascertain when the victims needed to report for Grand Jury testimony. Messages were left on their voicemail. On April 17, 2006, during the hours of 9:00 am and 11:30 am I again left messages for ASA Weiss and ASA Belohlavek for either of them to return my call as I had not heard from the State Attorney's Office as to the time and date of the Grand Jury.

At approximately 12:30 pm, I went to the State Attorney's Office and Located ASA Weiss and ASA Belohlavek in their offices. I entered ASA Belohlavek's office who informed me that she was going to return my call. She explained that an offer was made to the Defense, Atty Guy Fronstin and Atty Alan Dershowitz. The offer is 1 count of Agg Assault with intent to commit a felony, five years probation, with adjudication withheld. Epstein would have to submit to *psychiatric/sexual evaluation and no unsupervised visits with minors. When asked about all the other victims, ASA Belohlavek stated that was the only offer made as to one victim, [Mary]. ASA Belohlavek['s] cell phone rang and went to voice mail. She checked her voice mail and played the message on speaker. The caller identified himself as Atty Guy Fronstin and acknowledged the deal made between them. Fronstin stated in the message, he spoke with his client, Jeffrey Epstein, and would agree to this deal. Fronstin asked to call off the grand jury as they would accept this deal. Belohlavek stated a probable cause would be needed to book Epstein in the county Jail and would let me know as to when it was needed. I explained my disapproval of the deal and not being consulted prior to the deal being offered. However I expressed that was only my opinion and the final approval would come from the Chief of Police. She explained to have Chief Reiter call Barry Krischer about the deal. I left the area and returned to the police station where I briefed the Chief about the deal offered.*

I checked my voice mail messages and discovered a message from [the] stepmother for the victim [Mary]. She was calling because the State Attorney's Office still had not returned any of her calls as to when they are needed for this case. I then called ASA Belohlavek's office and left messages for her to call the victims on this case and explain to them what the State Attorney's Office had done.

CHAPTER 44

Michael Reiter: May 2006

A plea offer?

Chief Reiter is *outraged*. His team has logged thousands of hours of work. They've assembled mountains of evidence. But instead of going to trial, the state attorney wants to see Epstein get off with a misdemeanor, five years of probation, and a psych exam.

Why?

Alan Dershowitz has presented the prosecutors with his own pieces of evidence—printouts from the victims' Myspace pages.

In her "About Me" column, under "Best physical feature," Mary has written "Ass and eyes."

Under "Ever drank" and "Ever smoked pot," she's written "Yeah."

Under "Ever shoplifted": "Lots."

Under "Ever skinny dipped": "Yeah."

Under "[Do] you wanna lose your virginity": "I already lost it."

One of the victims has been caught with drugs and arrested. She's also been caught stealing from Victoria's

Secret. From the state attorney's perspective, these girls look like compromised women. And if what they say about Epstein is true, wouldn't that make them prostitutes?

As witnesses, they would be weak, while the lawyers on Epstein's side were exceptionally strong.

Alan Dershowitz had represented Claus von Bülow, the British socialite who was acquitted of the murder of his wife, Sunny. Dershowitz had been on O. J. Simpson's team when the former football star was acquitted of the murders of his ex-wife, Nicole Brown Simpson and Nicole's friend Ronald Lyle Goldman. And rich as von Bülow and Simpson had been, neither one had had the resources that Epstein was willing and able to deploy in his own defense.

Neither of them had been intimate friends with his lawyer.

As far as Reiter was concerned, none of that mattered. Even if Epstein thought that the girls he'd molested were eighteen years old—even if they had *lied* to him—it didn't matter under Florida law. The chief grew worried that in Epstein's case exceptions were being made, and he grew even more concerned with each unreturned call that he made to the state attorney's office.

On May 1, the Palm Beach PD asked the state attorney's office to issue an arrest warrant for Jeffrey Epstein.

That same day, Chief Reiter took the extraordinary step of writing Barry Krischer a letter all but demanding that he recuse himself from the case.

TOWN OF PALM BEACH
POLICE DEPARTMENT

A NATIONAL AND STATE ACCREDITED LAW ENFORCEMENT AGENCY

May 1, 2006

PERSONAL AND CONFIDENTIAL

Mr. Barry E. Krischer, State Attorney
Office of the State Attorney
Fifteenth Judicial Circuit
401 North Dixie Highway
West Palm Beach, FL 33401

Dear Mr. Krischer,

Please find enclosed the probable cause affidavits and case filing packages thus far resulting from the Palm Beach Police Department's investigation of Jeffrey Epstein, Sarah Kellen and Haley Robson. The submission of these documents are both in response to Assistant State Attorney Lanna Belohlavek's request for them and to serve as the Palm Beach Police Department's presentation for prosecution.

I know that you agree that it is our shared responsibility to seek justice and to serve the public interest by discharging our duties with fairness and accountability. I must renew my prior observation to you that I continue to find your office's treatment of these cases highly unusual. It is regrettable that I am forced to communicate in this manner but my most recent telephone calls to you and those of the lead detective to your assigned attorneys have been unanswered and messages remain unreturned.

After giving this much thought and consideration, I must urge you to examine the unusual course that your office's handling of this matter has taken and consider if good and sufficient reason exists to require your disqualification from the prosecution of these cases.

Sincerely,

Michael S. Reiter
Chief of Police

MSR:nt

CHAPTER 45

Videotaped Deposition of Michael Reiter in B.B. vs.
Epstein, *a civil lawsuit against Jeffrey Epstein:*
November 23, 2009

Q: At some point you sent a letter to state attorney
   Barry Krischer. Let me show you what we'll mark as
   exhibit 3. Let me give you a chance to read through
   this letter again to help refresh your recollection.

A: I've read it.

Q: At this point, in May of 2006, I'm assuming based
   on what you told us before that you had had some
   conversations with Barry Krischer directly...by
   phone—correct?—prior to this letter.

A: I had conversations in person and by phone.

Q: Okay. But nonetheless in May—May 1, 2006—you
   felt the need to write this letter; is that correct?

A: Yes.

Q: Can you tell us why?

A: Well, I felt the handling—and just continued to
   feel that the way the state attorney's office handled
   this case was extremely unusual. I knew that Mr.
   Krischer was making decisions about this case. I felt

that his objectivity was lacking, and I felt that the appropriate way, after reading the statute that governed the assignment of cases to other circuits—I felt that his action met the standard. I used some of the words from the statute in here. And I attempted to call him, and he wouldn't return my phone calls.

The detective attempted to contact—his contact in the state attorney's office, Lanna Belohlavek, however you pronounce that...and she wouldn't return his calls. So I wrote the letter in hope that he would think about his situation and realize that his objectivity was insufficient to prosecute the case and ask the governor to appoint someone else. And I felt like that was necessary for a fair prosecution of our case that had been submitted to him.

Q: Could you tell us, explain to us, why you felt that his objectivity may be lacking in regards to this prosecution...? In other words, what evidence did you see here, uncover, that you felt made it potentially nonobjective?

A: Well...when I first told him about the case, and I realized that it was a serious case, [that] there were multiple victims, [and] that the suspect was very well known, I told him about it. And we were—it was in person. I talked to him after a meeting that he and I were both involved in. And I had known him to be a victim advocate and to protect the rights of children. Well, I know that he even wrote a portion of the statute that addresses those issues. And when I told him originally, he said, "Let's go for it; this is an adult male in his fifties who's had sexual contact with children of the ages of the victims." He said this is somebody who we have to stop. And whatever we need, he said, in the state attorney's office, we have a unit that's equipped to investigate and prosecute these kinds of cases. And I didn't have too many facts early on when I talked with him, but I knew that there were multiple victims and to our detectives they were believable. So when time went on and Mr. Epstein became aware of the investigation and his lawyers contacted the state attorney's office, they told me that.

And from that point on, and I believe it was Mr. Dershowitz initially, the tone and tenor of the discussions of this case with Mr. Krischer changed completely. [At] one point he suggested that we write [Epstein] a notice to appear, which would be for a misdemeanor. He just completely changed from not only our first conversation about this[—when] he didn't know the name Jeffrey Epstein—till when he had been informed on Mr. Epstein's reputation and his wealth, and I just thought that very unusual.

I feel like I know him or knew him very well, the state attorney, and I just felt like he could not objectively make decisions about this case: that is why I wrote it.

CHAPTER 46

Detective Recarey: May 2006

Chief Reiter's letter to the state attorney had no per-
ceptible effect.

Krischer did not recuse himself from the case.
No arrest warrant was issued. And on the afternoon of
May 3, Detective Recarey received a telephone call from
assistant state attorney Daliah Weiss, who advised him
that she had been taken off the Epstein case.

Weiss had been the perfect person to prosecute
Epstein. As a member of the special victims unit, she
focused on sex crimes and crimes against children, prosecuting high-profile cases involving rape, aggravated
child abuse, and neglect. But Epstein had added another
lawyer, a man named Jack Goldberger, and made Goldberger his attorney of record.

Goldberger was friendly with Barry Krischer—and
an associate of Goldberger's was married to Daliah
Weiss.

If Epstein's legal team had wanted to remove Weiss
from the case, this would have been a good way to do it.

Nine days later, Detective Recarey met with ASA

Lanna Belohlavek, who told him that her boss, Barry Krischer, had asked her again to take the case to the grand jury. Recarey told Belohlavek that he had already requested arrest warrants for Epstein, Sarah Kellen, and Wendy Dobbs. The Palm Beach PD had finished its investigation months earlier, he said, and had been waiting since then for the case to move forward. He asked her once more to issue the warrants. Once again Belohlavek declined, saying that the original offer her office had made to Epstein's old lawyer had been resubmitted to the new lawyer. When Epstein's reply came, she would call.

While waiting for that call, Recarey received several calls from Mary's father, who told him that he was being followed by a green Chevrolet Monte Carlo—tailed so aggressively that other vehicles were being run off the road. Recarey ran the plates and found that the Chevy was registered to one Zachary Bechard of Jupiter, Florida.

Bechard was a licensed private eye.

"A funny thing happened in Palm Beach," says Tim Malloy, who was working as a TV newscaster in South Florida at the time.

"This would have been right around the time that Michael Reiter sent his letter asking Barry Krischer to recuse himself from the case. I didn't even know what Epstein looked like, really, at the time. We had pictures taken by the British tabloids, where the link to Prince Andrew first broke. But we didn't have too many of them. What we *did* have was a contact in the hangar where Epstein kept his 727.

"I don't know how much you know about Palm Beach International Airport. It's the kind of place that has private hangars, valet parking, and waiting lounges that look as chic as anything you'll see in Manhattan. It's an airport for the rich, basically. Saudi princes, heads of state. Powerful men who value their privacy. You can bring limousines onto the tarmac. And we found out Epstein was very secretive about his dealings there. He didn't want anyone to know the tail numbers on his planes.

"But our contact didn't like Epstein. And he was horrified by how young the girls around Epstein were. So thanks to him, we had the 727's tail number, and thanks to one other source—someone I won't say too much about here—we had Epstein's flight plan for a certain trip he was making. We knew he was going to land at the airport. And so our producer climbed into the station's traffic helicopter and told the pilot to hover at five hundred feet a quarter mile south of the field.

"Our cameraman had a telephoto lens. The idea was to get a tight shot, on video, of Epstein deplaning. And for a moment we *did* get the shot: Epstein, with the collar of his cashmere coat flipped up over his neck, about to run down the steps into a cart that was waiting for him.

"Then he saw our helicopter, with the station's markings.

"I was doing a live voice-over on Epstein's arrival. It was the first video anyone had on him up to that point. But Epstein had *run* back onto the plane. Then, during the next commercial break, my producer told me through my headpiece: 'Jeffrey Epstein wants us to stop taking his picture. In fact, he wants to talk to you.'

"The cameraman kept rolling. And eventually Epstein got out, got into a car with tinted windows, and was driven over the bridge to his home in Palm Beach. So in a sense we failed to get the story. But the fact that Epstein would call a news program from his plane and command them to order the program's traffic helicopter away—that says something about the man's arrogance. And maybe his temper."

CHAPTER 47

Mary: July 2006

On June 29, assistant state attorney Lanna Belohlavek told Detective Recarey that despite his protestations, the case would be going to a grand jury after all. One had been convened for July 19.

On July 12, Recarey spoke with Mary's stepmother, who said that she still hadn't heard from the state attorney's office. This, too, was odd, since Recarey knew that Mary would be called upon to testify.

She was back in Palm Beach now, after months of living with out-of-state relatives.

All in all, it had been a very tough year for Mary.

"What has happened to my daughter's life is criminal," her father would say.

Mary had been sent to a school for troubled children. For her it was the wrong place at the worst time in her life. She had gotten into more fights there, growing depressed and withdrawn from her sister and parents. Helplessly, her parents watched her spiral out of control. As they neared the end of their rope, they sent her out of state. But after the move, Mary had fallen apart completely. She used drugs, fell in with a bad crowd, ran away from her relatives, and shacked up with a gang of drug dealers.

When the gang was busted by local police, the dealers blamed Mary for snitching and put out the word that they wanted her dead.

"We had to move her again," Mary's father explained. "We finally got her into therapy—she's still seeing the therapist. And worst of all, she developed HPV. She's already had to have a serious operation."

Mary's troubles didn't end there. On June 28, she was brought in front of the grand jury. She hadn't been briefed by the state attorney—she hadn't even *met* the prosecutors—and she had no idea what she would be asked.

Almost immediately, she found that she was being treated more like a criminal than like a witness or victim.

"The prosecutor produced a printout of our daughter's Myspace page," Mary's father recalls. "Mary was stunned. She began to cry. The prosecutor accused her of all sort of things; it was like she was *working* for Epstein.

"All this time, we knew that we were being watched. Creepy guys. Private investigators from Miami. They would follow us, scaring the hell out of my wife and Mary's sister. My car was vandalized. It was like living in hell."

By this point, Epstein's defense dream team included Jack Goldberger, Alan Dershowitz, and Gerald Lefcourt. All of them had excellent track records. Dershowitz and Lefcourt were two of America's most famous lawyers, and before long, another celebrity lawyer—Ken Starr, the former solicitor general who had had Bill Clinton impeached for perjury—would join Epstein's team.

As far as Mary's parents were concerned, their daughter had walked into an ambush. *Everyone* in the courtroom seemed to be playing defense on the side of Jeffrey Epstein. And as for the second girl—Alison, who claimed that she had been raped—she never testified in court at all.

CHAPTER 48

Michael Reiter: July 2006

On July 28, the grand jury reached a verdict that floored the Palm Beach PD.

The original plea deal that Krischer had offered to Epstein had been bad enough. Now the grand jury was recommending that Epstein be charged with just one felony count of solicitation of prostitution.

There was no mention of underage girls. The original accusation—four felony counts of unlawful sex acts with minors and one felony count of lewd and lascivious molestation—had simply evaporated.

It wasn't enough to send Epstein to prison.

Epstein was allowed to surrender on a Sunday, when no one would know he'd been arraigned. A few hours later, he was released on three thousand dollars bail.

The Palm Beach PD was not even notified.

Once again, Chief Reiter was outraged. So much so that he took the extraordinary step of calling the FBI and the federal prosecutor's office.

At the time, the federal prosecutor of the Southern District of Florida was a Republican named R. Alexander

Acosta. Chief Reiter recalls being present at Acosta's swearing-in ceremony and remembers Acosta's declaration that one of his goals would be the prosecution, to the fullest extent of the law, of anyone who takes advantage of the weak—especially perpetrators of sex crimes. Disgusted with Krischer's laissez-faire attitude, Reiter recalls thinking he'd found his man.

In Acosta, the chief saw a prosecutor who wouldn't shy away from confronting a man with Jeffrey Epstein's resources and connections.

But it turned out that Acosta had worked under Ken Starr at Starr's high-powered multinational law firm, Kirkland & Ellis. And while Acosta had a sterling résumé, which included a stint clerking for future Supreme Court justice Samuel Alito, he had only argued two cases before a judge.

At the time, Reiter did not know this. All he knew was that someone had to look much more seriously into Jeffrey Epstein's crimes.

Reiter's actions did not necessarily make him a hero—at least, not in *every* corner of the community he served.

"I had individuals suggest that the department's approach to the investigation and my referral of the investigation to the FBI was more horsepower than the investigation deserved. And I had other individuals suggest that—yeah, the term 'back off' probably fits," Reiter said in his deposition for *B.B. vs. Epstein*.

"I had people in the community in Palm Beach who either made comments directly to me or to others who relayed them to me that I didn't need to take the tack in the investigation that we did, which is [to] completely investigate it and then refer it to the FBI after the state case was resolved," Reiter said in the deposition. "I had one individual who came to see me a couple of times about this."

According to the chief, the individual in question was a prominent Palm Beach politician.

"He said this wasn't necessary; this was a case that was really very minor," Reiter recalled. "The victims had lifestyles that don't make them—shouldn't make them believable to the police department."

"I told him that those kinds of suggestions to me were improper and he should stop," said Reiter. "That he had taken a couple of steps down the road toward something that could eventually constitute a crime. We talked several times. Early on it didn't end favorably. You know, this is an individual [whom] I had to interact with in my official capacity and in his official capacity as well."

The Palm Beach politician wasn't the only one to pressure the police chief. "I received comments from a variety of different viewpoints...in some cases I had people tell me, hey, he's a Palm Beacher, why are you investigating a Palm Beacher?" Reiter would say when deposed. "I had people that said it was an unfavorable career move for me to ask the state attorney to remove himself from the case and to refer it to the FBI....I had plenty of people that told me that that was a mistake."

Reiter didn't back off. To have done so would have been a betrayal—not only of the victims but also of his vocation and the community he had sworn he would serve.

"My responsibility was to protect everyone that lives in Palm Beach and preserve their constitutional rights and be the police department for all," Reiter said. "And I think that under the law, particularly under the criminal laws, that all people have to, by the nature of our system, be treated exactly alike."

But along with handing the case off to the FBI and the US attorney, Reiter took another unusual step. He wrote personal letters—on Palm Beach PD letterhead—to the parents of the victims in the case.

He delivered the letters by hand.

TOWN OF PALM BEACH
POLICE DEPARTMENT

A NATIONAL AND STATE ACCREDITED LAW ENFORCEMENT AGENCY

July 24, 2006

HAND DELIVERED

Dear Mr ▮

Your daughter ▮ was the victim of a crime which has been investigated by the Palm Beach Police Department and subsequently referred for prosecution to the Palm Beach County State Attorney's Office. You may be aware that Jeffrey Epstein was indicted on charges of solicitation for prostitution by a State of Florida grand jury last week and turned himself in at the Palm Beach County jail on July 23, 2006. While I do not speak for them, it is my understanding that it is the full context in which the Palm Beach County State Attorney's Office intends to address the charges that involved the crime in which your daughter was victim.

Please know that it is the role and responsibility of law enforcement to investigate crime and to refer appropriate charges to the prosecutor for consideration. I believe that the Palm Beach Police Department has acted competently and responsibly in carrying out this role. Should you have any questions concerning the state prosecution of this matter, they are best addressed by the Palm Beach County State Attorney's Office.

I do not feel that justice has been sufficiently served by the indictment that has been issued. Therefore, please know that his matter has been referred to the Federal Bureau of Investigation to determine if violations of federal law have occurred. In the event that the FBI should choose to pursue this matter, the Palm Beach Police Department will assist them in their investigation of potential violations of federal law.

Please feel free to contact me at (561) 838-5460 should you have any questions.

Sincerely,

Michael S. Reiter
Chief of Police

MSR:nt

CHAPTER 49

Jeffrey Epstein: September 2007

In the winter of 2013, Scott Blake, a forty-seven-year-old middle school principal from Palm Beach Gardens, Florida, would be sentenced to the minimum mandatory sentence—ten years in prison, with ten years of probation on top—for pleading guilty to one charge of soliciting sex with a minor.

Blake's crime? He sent sexually charged messages to a Boynton Beach police officer who was pretending to be a fifteen-year-old boy. But in a sense, Blake was lucky: he could have been sentenced to life. The case was an interesting example of the kind of treatment regular Florida folks could expect just for *soliciting* sex with a minor. But nothing about Jeffrey Epstein was regular—and the plea deal he managed to strike in 2007 was simply *extraordinary*.

Epstein had bought himself one of the best defense teams ever assembled. His connections and contributions to Democratic causes had made him a player on that side of the political aisle. He had a famous Republican, Bill Clinton's nemesis, Ken Starr, working the other side. And just to make sure they'd covered the bases, Epstein's team also recruited Roy Black—the lawyer who'd cleared William Kennedy Smith of rape and kept Rush Limbaugh out of prison for his alleged illegal drug use—and Jay Lefkowitz, a defense attorney who'd worked with US attorney R. Alexander Acosta at Ken Starr's law firm.

And so in September, the US attorney's office reached a formal agreement with Epstein's team: the United States would defer federal prosecution in favor of prosecution by the state of Florida.

A non-prosecution agreement (NPA) was drafted; among other things, it assured Epstein that he would not be prosecuted in the Southern District of Florida for felony offenses involving the sexual abuse of underage girls. (By that point, thirty known victims had been discovered.) Instead it allowed him to plead guilty to state felony offenses for solicitation of prostitution and the procurement of minors for prostitution. The NPA established a procedure that allowed Epstein's victims to sue him in civil court and took the extraordinary step of ensuring that "any potential co-conspirators" of Epstein's would be immune from prosecution.

"In consideration of Epstein's agreement to plead guilty and to provide compensation in the manner described above, if Epstein successfully fulfills all of the terms and conditions of this agreement, the United States also agrees that it will not institute any criminal charges against any potential co-conspirators of Epstein," the agreement stated, mentioning Sarah Kellen and Nadia Marcinkova by name.

"The parties anticipate that this agreement will not be made part of any public record," the document concludes. "If the United States receives a Freedom of Information Act request or any compulsory process commanding the disclosure of the agreement, it will provide notice to Epstein before making that disclosure."

Remarkably, despite assurances they'd received from the feds, none of the victims was consulted prior to the drafting of this NPA.

If Epstein did not sign the agreement, he faced a fifty-seven-count indictment and a decade or more in prison. But Epstein's team of lawyers had gotten him a deal so sweet it could have rotted all the teeth in South Florida.

For all his protestations of innocence, there was every reason in the world to agree to an NPA.

On September 24, 2007, Epstein did sign it.

Once again, none of the victims had been consulted or notified.

CHAPTER 50

Jane Doe: February 2008

As a result of the non-prosecution agreement, a fifty-three-count indictment that federal prosecutors had prepared against Jeffrey Epstein—one that claimed he'd abused dozens of underage women—never was filed.

But as far as lawyers representing Epstein's victims were concerned, the fact that those victims were not consulted about the non-prosecution agreement was inexcusable. The "government deliberately kept crime victims 'in the dark' so that it could enter into a plea arrangement designed to prevent the victims from raising any objections," they would argue, in documents filed on February 10, 2016. For nine months, the lawyers claimed, from the time that the NPA was signed, on September 24, 2007, Krischer's office, "doing Epstein's bidding, [had] concealed the NPA's existence from victim[s]" and continued to do so until the moment that Epstein had to plead guilty in court, which he finally did June 30, 2008.

In the interim, according to their lawyers, Epstein's

victims were only told, "This case is currently under investigation."

A lawsuit that Bradley Edwards, a victims' rights attorney in Fort Lauderdale, filed in July of 2008 cited the Crime Victims' Rights Act, or CVRA (title 18, section 3771, of the US Code), which states that "victims of federal crimes have rights, including the right to be heard in court, and most particularly, not to be precluded from court proceedings, and the right to be treated fairly."

According to him, prosecutors had violated the CVRA rights of the victims. Edwards, who said he was working pro bono, knew that this suit against the government would not allow for monetary recovery of any sort (including lawyers' fees). But he also knew that if the government, urged by Jeffrey Epstein, had entered into a contract that improperly or illegally violated the rights of Epstein's victims, then that contract, by nature, would have been improper in and of itself—in which case, the only remedy would have been to have the contract invalidated. And while it is difficult to know what, exactly, would happen if the contract *is* overturned, one possibility is that the government could prosecute Epstein for crimes against his victims, if the statute of limitations on those crimes has not expired.

At the time of this writing, that case is winding its way through the courts. It has all the earmarks of a modern-day *Bleak House*—the Charles Dickens novel about a legal case that is so massive and so complex that it drags on forever and drags everyone involved into the mire.

In the meantime, Epstein began to settle out of court with his victims.

In February of 2008, a Virginia woman who went by

the alias Jane Doe #2 brought a fifty-million-dollar law-suit against Epstein.

At the time of their meeting, she claimed, Epstein was fifty-two years old. She was a teenager, and her complaint, which was made public, gave the rest of the world an early glimpse of what Epstein, and the inner workings of his secret world, looked like from a victim's perspective.

"Epstein is a financier and money manager with a secret clientele limited exclusively to billionaires," the lawsuit alleged. "He is himself a man of tremendous wealth, power and influence. He maintains his principal home in New York and also owns residences in New Mexico, St. Thomas and Palm Beach, FL. The allegations herein concern Epstein's conduct while at his lavish estate in Palm Beach." The complaint continued:

> *Upon information and belief, Epstein has a sexual preference and obsession for underage minor girls. He engaged in a plan and scheme in which he gained access to primarily economically disadvantaged minor girls in his home, sexually assaulted these girls, and then gave them money. In or about 2004–2005, Jane Doe, then approximately 16 years old, fell into Epstein's trap and became one of his victims.*
>
> *Upon information and belief, Jeffrey Epstein carried out his schemes and assaulted girls in Florida, New York, and on his private Island, known as Little St. James, in St. Thomas.*
>
> *Epstein's scheme involved the use of young girls to recruit underage girls. (Upon information and belief, the young girl who brought Jane Doe to Epstein was herself a minor victim of Epstein, and will therefore not be named in this Complaint.) Under Epstein's plan, underage girls were recruited ostensibly to*

give a wealthy man a massage for monetary compensation in his Palm Beach mansion. The recruiter would be contacted when Epstein was planning to be at his Palm Beach residence or soon after he had arrived there. Epstein or someone on his behalf would direct the recruiter to bring one or more underage girls to the residence. The recruiter, upon information and belief, generally sought out economically disadvantaged underaged girls from western Palm Beach County who would be enticed by the money being offered—generally $200 to $300 per "massage" session—and who were perceived as less likely to complain to authorities or have credibility if allegations of improper conduct were made. This was an important element of Epstein's plan.

Epstein's plan reflected a particular pattern and method. Upon arrival at Epstein's mansion, the underaged victim would be introduced to Sarah Kellen, Epstein's assistant, who gathered the girl's personal information, including her name and telephone number. Ms. Kellen would then bring the girl up a flight of stairs to a bedroom that contained a massage table in addition to other furnishings. There were photographs of nude women lining the stairway hall and in the bedroom. The girl would then find herself alone in the room with Epstein, who would be wearing only a towel. He would then remove his towel and lie naked on the massage table, and direct the girl to remove her clothes. Epstein would then perform one or more lewd, lascivious and sexual acts, including masturbation and touching the girl's vagina.

Consistent with the foregoing plan and scheme, Jane Doe was recruited to give Epstein a massage for monetary compensation. Jane was brought to Epstein's mansion in Palm Beach. Once at the mansion, Jane was introduced to Sarah Kellen, who led her up the flight of stairs to the room with the massage table. In this room, Epstein told Jane to take off her clothes and give him a massage. Jane kept her panties and bra on and complied with Epstein's instructions. Epstein wore only a towel around his waste [sic]. After a short period of time, Epstein removed the towel and rolled over exposing his penis. Epstein began to masturbate and he sexually assaulted Jane.

After Epstein had completed the assault, Jane was then able to get dressed, leave the room and go back down the stairs. Jane was paid $200 by Epstein. The young girl who recruited Jane was paid $100 by Epstein for bringing Jane to him.

As a result of this encounter with Epstein, Jane experienced confusion, shame, humiliation and embarrassment, and has suffered severe psychological and emotional injuries.

CHAPTER 51

Jeffrey Epstein: June 30, 2008

On June 30, 2008, more than three years after the start of Officer Pagan's investigation into his dealings with underage girls, Jeffrey Epstein reported to the Palm Beach County jail.

A few days earlier, Epstein had taken a phone call from the *New York Times*. At the time, he'd been working, or vacationing (the line having long since blurred), at his compound on Little Saint Jeff's.

"I respect the legal process," Epstein had said. "I will abide by this."

He'd spent years fighting the charges—fighting the state, then the federal government, in an effort to avoid a sentence that would have seen him emerge from prison an old man. But the battle had aged him. *Mellowed* him, even. Months earlier, he had all but boasted to a journalist from *New York* magazine.

"It's the Icarus story, someone who flies too close to the sun," that journalist said in reference to "the agony" of Epstein's legal "ordeal."

"Did Icarus like massages?" Epstein responded.

But after Epstein's indictment, there were no more boasts. For the most part, he kept silent in public and retreated into his *Eyes Wide Shut* world. And when the *New York Times* did manage to get him to speak on the record, he spoke like a chastened man.

Sitting on his patio down on Little St. James, Epstein likened himself to the shipwrecked Gulliver after he washes ashore on Lilliput.

"Gulliver's playfulness had unintended consequences," he said.

On the eve of his departure, he had a few more things to say:

"That is what happens with wealth. There are unexpected burdens as well as benefits...."

"Your body can be confined, but not your mind...."

"I am not blameless...."

Outside of the agreement he'd signed with the prosecutor's office, this was the closest Epstein had come to admitting his guilt. But strange details were sprinkled throughout the story. He had formed a "board of directors of friends" who would counsel him on his behavior. And, seemingly for the first time, he'd hired a full-time masseur—a man.

Readers of the *New York Times* might have wondered: Epstein was going to jail for eighteen months. What need would he have for a full-time masseur?

The story's last line hinted at the answer: in preparation for incarceration, Epstein had set up an e-mail alert.

From then on, his automatic reply would read "On vacation."

PART V

Incarceration

CHAPTER 52

Jeffrey Epstein: June 30, 2008

The Palm Beach County Main Detention Center is on the west side of Lake Worth Lagoon, which separates West Palm Beach from the island of Palm Beach. Epstein's home on El Brillo Way is five miles to the east. Mary's high school is several miles to the west.

It's fitting, somehow, that this jail—which is the jail Epstein ends up in, after turning himself in to the local sheriff—lies in between the two points.

The detention center's inmates, their families, and their lawyers call it the Gun Club, a reference not only to the jail's address, on Gun Club Road, but also to its population of hustlers, burglars, drug dealers, rapists, and murderers. There's the occasional hooker as well. And, from time to time, Haitian refugees are lodged there.

There are three thousand inmates in all.

Some wait a year before making their way to the courthouse, their date with the public defender, and an appearance before the judge. Some get out much sooner, if only they can make bail. But there's no bail without money—or at least collateral—and, of course, being without money is often what lands people in jail in the first place.

Jeffrey Epstein could have posted bail for every single inmate in the Gun Club.

But that's just one of the ways in which Epstein is unlike his fellow inmates. He's an admitted pedophile now. Even a famous one.

And, famously, pedophiles tend to fare poorly in jail.

Luckily for Epstein, Ric Bradshaw, the sheriff in charge of local jails, transfers Epstein to the infirmary, where he spends exactly one night before being transferred seven miles up the road to a much smaller, safer location: the Palm Beach County *Central* Detention Center—or, as it's known, the Stockade.

"It's not somewhere we'd put a serial killer," Ric Bradshaw says.

Most of the residents here are addicts who take part in drug education programs, prostitutes, petty criminals, and drunks. It's a far safer place for Epstein to be, and, unlike other inmates (except, of course, those being held in solitary), he'll end up with his own cell, even his own wing, which he has to himself. Epstein's allowed to pay for a security guard, who sits outside the cell and keeps watch. And he's allowed any number of visitors.

For a convicted felon, it's an extraordinary benefits package.

But according to Sheriff Bradshaw, who also oversees the Stockade, Epstein is incredulous over the treatment he is receiving.

"He was astonished that he had to go to prison at all," Bradshaw remembers.

"Let's just say he didn't think he belonged there."

CHAPTER 53

Sheriff Ric Bradshaw: June 2015

O**ur job," says Ric Bradshaw, "was to make sure nobody killed him."**

Sheriff Bradshaw could have stepped off the set of a Western. Imposingly tall, with his cowboy hat, Kurt Russell mustache, and slow, southern drawl, he looks *exactly* like an old-school law officer—the kind you once would have found patrolling the streets of Tombstone, Deadwood, or Dodge City. He's been a lawman for forty-four years, eleven of which have been spent as the head of the county's jails. As a rule, he doesn't talk to the media, and today, as he talks about Jeffrey Epstein, he's clearly uncomfortable, fidgety, and ill disposed.

But here in his wood-paneled office on the first floor of the Gun Club, Bradshaw remembers Epstein quite well.

"We have a thousand sexual predators in the county," he says. "When he arrived here, he was one of them. He definitely fit the category we have to ensure the general population is not going to take their anger out on."

Although he understands that Epstein is a sex

offender and has a sense of the scope of his alleged crimes, Bradshaw's also aware that the actual *conviction* was for a "low-level felony." At the request of Epstein's attorneys—a request that is confirmed by a court order—Epstein is quickly granted "work release."

What it means in practice is that six days a week, for up to sixteen—sixteen!—hours each day, Epstein is allowed to leave the Stockade to be driven by a designated driver in a car earmarked especially for him to any one of three places: his lawyer Jack Goldberger's office in downtown West Palm Beach, the Palm Beach office of a science foundation that he's established, and his house on El Brillo Way.

Despite the ankle bracelet he wears, it could be argued that as a fabulously rich prisoner with two of his own jets parked nearby, at the Palm Beach International Airport, Epstein might have posed a flight risk.

Instead, every day of the week save one, he's allowed to go to his lawyer's, to go to his office, or simply to go home.

Did the deputy in charge of Epstein go to the house on El Brillo Way?

Ric Bradshaw considers the question.

"Yes," he says, "he did."

Did the deputy go inside the house?

"Yes, he did."

If so, the deputy might have encountered Nadia Marcinkova, who was staying on El Brillo Way at the time. He may also have met a suave short-haired gentleman who spoke with a distinct French accent.

That would be Jean-Luc Brunel.

For the duration of Jeffrey Epstein's stay—or half stay—in the Stockade, Brunel's taken up residence in the house on El Brillo Way.

CHAPTER 54

Jeffrey Epstein: June 30, 2008–July 21, 2009

According to Sheriff Ric Bradshaw, the treatment Jeffrey Epstein received in the Stockade was not preferential. By some measures, he isn't wrong.

In 2010, millionaire polo mogul John Goodman killed a young man while driving drunk. He was convicted but was allowed to spend two years under house arrest while his appeal was being tried.

Like Epstein, Goodman was allowed visitors. But Goodman's visitor list was nothing like Jeffrey Epstein's.

Nadia Marcinkova is said to have visited Epstein in jail more than seventy times.

Epstein's assistant Sarah Kellen also visited Epstein in the Stockade.

A Russian mixed martial artist named Igor "Houdini" Zinoviev was another visitor, as was a disbarred lawyer and financial fraudster named Arnold Prosperi, whose own prison sentence had been commuted by Bill Clinton on the day before Clinton left office.

Sheriff Bradshaw wants to be clear: none of these visits was conjugal.

But even US attorney Acosta, who negotiated Epstein's unusual agreement with the government, would say that Epstein's arrangement was highly irregular.

"Epstein appears to have received highly unusual treatment while in jail," Acosta would say in a letter addressed to the general public. "Although the terms of confinement in a state prison are a matter appropriately left to the state of Florida and not federal authorities, without doubt, the treatment that he received while in state custody undermined the purpose of a jail sentence."

And, of course, Epstein's stay at the Stockade was subsidized by taxpayers.

CHAPTER 55

*R. Alexander Acosta's letter to the general public,
March 20, 2011*

To whom it may concern:

I served as U. S. Attorney for the Southern District of Florida from 2005 through 2009. Over the past weeks, I have read much regarding Mr. Jeffrey Epstein. Some appears true, some appears distorted. I thought it appropriate to provide some background, with two caveats: (i) under Justice Department guidelines, I cannot discuss privileged internal communications among department attorneys and (ii) I no longer have access to the original documents, and as the matter is now nearly 4 years old, the precision of memory is reduced.

The Epstein matter was originally presented to the Palm Beach County State Attorney. Palm Beach Police alleged that Epstein unlawfully hired underage high-school females to provide him sexually lewd and erotic massages. Police sought felony charges that would have resulted in a term of imprisonment. According to press reports, however, in 2006 the State Attorney, in part due to concerns regarding the quality of the evidence, agreed to charge Epstein only with one count of aggravated assault with no intent to commit a felony. That charge would have resulted in no jail time, no requirement to register as a sexual offender and no restitution for the underage victims.

Local police were dissatisfied with the State Attorney's conclusions, and requested a federal investigation. Federal authorities received the State's evidence and engaged in additional investigation. Prosecutors weighed the quality of the evidence and the likelihood for success at trial. With a federal case, there were two additional considerations. First, a federal criminal prosecution requires that the crime be more than local; it must have an interstate nexus. Second, as the matter was initially charged by the state, the federal responsibility is, to some extent, to back-stop state authorities to ensure that there is no miscarriage of justice, and not to also prosecute federally that which has already been charged at the state level.

After considering the quality of the evidence and the additional considerations, prosecutors concluded that the state charge was insufficient. In early summer 2007, the prosecutors and agents in this case met with Mr. Epstein's attorney, Roy Black. Mr. Black is perhaps best known for his successful defense of William Kennedy Smith. The prosecutors presented Epstein a choice: plead to more serious state felony charges (that would result in 2 years' imprisonment, registration as a sexual offender, and restitution for the victims) or else prepare for a federal felony trial.

What followed was a year-long assault on the prosecution and the prosecutors. I use the word assault intentionally, as the defense in this case was more aggressive than any which I, or the prosecutors in my office, had previously encountered. Mr. Epstein hired an army of legal superstars: Harvard Professor Alan Dershowitz, former Judge and then Pepperdine Law Dean Kenneth Starr, former Deputy Assistant to the President and then Kirkland & Ellis Partner Jay Lefkowitz, and several others, including prosecutors who had formerly worked in the U.S. Attorney's Office and in the Child Exploitation and Obscenity Section of the Justice Department. Defense attorneys next requested a meeting with me to challenge the prosecution and the terms previously presented by the prosecutors in their meeting with Mr. Black. The prosecution team and I met with defense counsel in Fall 2007, and I reaffirmed the office's position: two years, registration and restitution, or trial.

Over the next several months, the defense team presented argument after argument claiming that felony criminal proceedings against Epstein were unsupported by the evidence and lacked a basis in law, and that the office's insistence on jail-time was motivated by a zeal to overcharge a man merely because he is wealthy. They bolstered their arguments with legal opinions from well-known legal experts. One member of the defense team warned me that the office's excess zeal in forcing a good man to serve time in jail might be the subject of a book if we continued to proceed with the matter. My office systematically considered and rejected each argument, and when we did, my office's decisions were appealed to Washington. As to the warning, I ignored it.

The defense strategy was not limited to legal issues. Defense counsel investigated individual prosecutors and their families, looking for personal peccadilloes that may provide a basis for disqualification. Disqualifying a prosecutor is an effective (though rarely used) strategy, as eliminating the individuals most familiar with the facts and thus most qualified to take a case to trial harms likelihood for success. Defense counsel tried to disqualify at least two prosecutors. I carefully reviewed, and then rejected, these arguments.

Despite the army of attorneys, the office held firm to the terms first presented to Mr. Black in the original meeting. On June 30, 2008, after yet another last minute appeal to Washington D.C. was rejected, Epstein pled guilty in state court. He was to serve 18 months imprisonment, register as a sexual offender for life, and provide restitution to the victims.

Some may feel that the prosecution should have been tougher. Evidence that has come to light since 2007 may encourage that view. Many victims have since spoken out, filing detailed statements in civil cases seeking damages. Physical evidence has since been discovered. Had these additional statements and evidence been known, the outcome may have been different. But they were not known to us at the time.

A prosecution decision must be based on admissible facts known at the time. In cases of this type, those are unusually difficult because victims are frightened and often decline to testify or if they do speak, they give contradictory statements. Our judgment in this case, based on the evidence known at the time, was that it was better to have a billionaire serve time in jail, register as a sex offender, and pay his victims restitution than risk a trial with a reduced likelihood of success. I supported that judgment then, and based on the state law as it then stood and the evidence known at the time, I would support that judgment again.

Epstein's treatment, while in state custody, likewise may encourage the view that the office should have been tougher. Although the terms of confinement in a state prison are a matter appropriately left to the State of Florida, and not federal authorities, without doubt, the treatment that he received while in state custody undermined the purpose of a jail sentence.

Some may also believe that the prosecution should have been tougher in retaliation for the defense's tactics. The defense, arguably, often failed to negotiate in good faith. They would obtain concessions as part of a negotiation and agree to proceed, only to change their minds, and appeal the office's position to Washington. The investigations into the family lives of individual prosecutors were, in my opinion, uncalled for, as were the accusations of bias and/or misconduct against individual prosecutors. At times, some prosecutors felt that we should just go to trial, and at times I felt that frustration myself. What was right in the first meeting, however, remained right irrespective of defense tactics. Individuals have a constitutional right to a defense. The aggressive exercise of that right should not be punished, nor should a defense counsel's exercise of their right to appeal a U.S Attorney to Washington D.C. Prosecutors must be careful not to allow frustration and anger with defense counsel to influence their judgment.

After the plea, I recall receiving several phone calls. One was from the FBI Special Agent-In-Charge. He called to offer congratulations. He had been at many of the meetings regarding this case. He was aware of the tactics of the defense, and he called to praise our prosecutors for holding firm against the likes of Messrs. Black, Dershowitz, Lefkowitz and Starr. It was a proud moment. I also received calls or communications from Messrs. Dershowitz, Lefkowitz and Starr. I had known all three individuals previously, from my time in law school and at Kirkland & Ellis in the mid 90s. They all sought to make peace. I agreed to talk and meet with each of them after Epstein pled guilty, as I think it important that prosecutors battle defense attorneys in a case and then move on. I have tried, yet I confess that this has been difficult to do fully in this case.

The bottom line is this: Mr. Jeffrey Epstein, a billionaire, served time in jail and is now a registered sexual offender. He has been required to pay his victims restitution, though restitution clearly cannot compensate for the crime. And we know much more today about his crimes because victims have come forward to speak out. Some may disagree with prosecutorial judgments made in this case, but those individuals are not the ones who at the time reviewed the evidence available for trial and assessed the likelihood of success.

Respectfully,
R. Alexander Acosta
Former U.S. Attorney
Southern District of Florida

PART VI

Aftermath

CHAPTER 56

Jeffrey Epstein: July 2009

Jeffrey Epstein walks out of the Stockade on July 21, 2009, having served less than thirteen months of his eighteen-month sentence. One of the concessions his lawyers have gotten while working out his plea-deal guarantees is that the media not be alerted to the time and day of his departure.

But from now on, Epstein, who is fifty-six, will carry the mark of a level 3 sex offender—level 1 being the lowest, and level 3 indicating the highest possible risk of a future criminal act of a sexual nature. Wherever he goes, he will be forced to register as such.

Every ninety days, Epstein will have to check in with the authorities. Every year, the New York City Police Department will take his mug shot. And for a full year, Epstein will be under house arrest in Palm Beach.

This last prohibition doesn't stop him from flying, with court approval, on his own planes to New York and to Little Saint Jeff's, where the locals have taken to referring to Epstein's 727 as the Lolita Express.

There are other restrictions, of course, that Epstein is

supposed to abide by. He has to provide the state of Florida with a list of all the motor vehicles, boats, and airplanes he owns. The full list includes two Escalades, six Suburbans, two Ford F-150s, two Harley-Davidsons, a Land Rover, a Hummer H2, a thirty-four-foot JVC boat, and a thirty-five-foot Donzi powerboat.

Three of his five planes turn out to be registered to a company called Air Ghislaine, Inc.

As a registered sex offender, Epstein is legally obliged to undergo psychiatric treatment. This is a restriction he'll get around by having his own psychologist submit a report to law enforcement officers.

Epstein is also prohibited from accessing pornography on the Internet and using social networking for sexual purposes.

For Jeffrey Epstein, there will be no Bangbros, Tinder, or Swingles.com.

There *will* be lawsuits.

Six weeks before probation ends, he settles with seven women who sue him in civil court. But Epstein can easily afford the settlement payments. He won't be going back to jail, and in regard to further prosecution for any criminal actions, his troubles are behind him.

Not everyone who's spent time in his company will be so lucky.

CHAPTER 57

Alfredo Rodriguez: August 2009

Epstein's houseman, Alfredo Rodriguez, also ends up with a prison sentence.

In a sworn statement, Rodriguez talks about Epstein's maid, Lupita, who had complained to him about having to clean up after Epstein's "massages." Lupita, who was a devout Catholic, had cried as she described the stained towel and sex toys.

Rodriguez was fired by Epstein, he says, when he called 911 after seeing a strange car—a "beater"—in Epstein's driveway.

As it turned out, the car had belonged to one of Epstein's masseuses.

On his way out of the house on El Brillo Way, he took some of Epstein's papers, which he failed to produce when questioned by Chief Reiter's investigators.

For years, Rodriguez tried and failed to find work as a house manager. No one wanted to hire someone who'd worked for Jeffrey Epstein. Finally, desperately, he tried to sell the information he'd stolen.

The papers named underage girls and the places

where Epstein had taken them. The list included locations in California, Paris, New Mexico, New York, and Michigan. The papers also included the names, addresses, and phone numbers of famous individuals—Henry Kissinger, Mick Jagger, Dustin Hoffman, Ralph Fiennes, David Koch, Ted Kennedy, Donald Trump, Bill Richardson, Bill Clinton, and former Israeli prime minister Ehud Barak among them.

This was intriguing, if not at all damning. Epstein made a habit of collecting such information for future use. But information pertaining to the girls would have bolstered the state's case against Jeffrey Epstein, and by withholding it from the Palm Beach PD and the FBI, Rodriguez had committed a crime.

In his defense, Rodriguez would say that the papers were an "insurance policy." Without them, he believed, Epstein would have made him "disappear."

But now Rodriguez needed the money. And so a few weeks after Epstein's release from the Stockade, he approached a lawyer who was representing some of Epstein's masseuses. He had the "holy grail," he insisted. A "golden nugget." The names of hundreds of girls, he said, who had been abused by Epstein.

The lawyer told Rodriguez in no uncertain terms that he was obliged to turn whatever he had over to the authorities. By demanding money for the information, Rodriguez was committing another crime.

According to a sworn statement by Christina Pryor, a special agent with the FBI, Rodriguez "persisted that he would only turn over the information in his possession in exchange for $50,000."

Two months later, on October 28, the lawyer called Rodriguez, who insisted once more on being paid for the information. The lawyer told him that an associate would be in touch.

What the lawyer knew and Rodriguez did not know was that the associate in question was an undercover employee (UCE) of the FBI. A few days later, on November 2, the UCE calls Rodriguez and sets up a meeting, which takes place the following day.

"During the meeting, Rodriguez produced a small bound book and several sheets of legal pad paper containing handwritten notes," Special Agent Pryor would say in her statement. She continues:

Rodriguez explained that he had taken the bound book from his former employer's residence while employed there in 2004 to 2005 and that the book had been created by persons working for his former employer. Rodriguez discussed in detail the information within the book and identified important information to the UCE. In addition, Rodriguez admitted he had previously lied to the FBI. Rodriguez asked the UCE about the $50,000, took possession of the money, and began counting it.

Rodriguez was then detained for Obstruction of Official Proceedings, Title 18, U.S. Code, Section 1512(c), and questioned. After Miranda warnings were administered by agents, Rodriguez waived his rights and signed a written waiver of those rights. Rodriguez admitted that he had the documents and book in his possession and had never turned them over to local law enforcement or the FBI. In addition, Rodriguez advised he had witnessed nude girls whom he believed were underage at the pool area of his former employer's home, knew that his former employer was engaging in sexual contact with underage girls, and had viewed pornographic images of underage girls on computers in his employer's home. Rodriguez was then released from custody for further investigation.

The items that Rodriguez had attempted to sell to the UCE for $50,000.00 were reviewed by an agent familiar with the underlying criminal investigation. As Rodriguez had described, the items contained information material to the underlying investigation that would have been extremely useful in investigati[ng] and prosecuting the case, including the names and contact information of material witnesses and additional victims. Had those items been produced in response to the inquiries of the state law enforcement officers or the FBI Special Agents, their contents would have been presented to the federal grand jury.

Following his release, Alfredo Rodriguez was arrested again. He appeared in court on June 18, 2010, facing charges of corruptly concealing records and documents. Dressed in a blue jumpsuit and shackles, he apologized for his crimes and asked the court to be merciful.

He received a sentence of eighteen months.

It was the same punishment that Jeffrey Epstein had gotten for his crimes. But unlike Epstein, Alfredo Rodriguez served his time in a federal prison and did not ask for, or receive, permission to go on work release.

CHAPTER 58

Prince Andrew: 2011

Prince Andrew also fares poorly in the wake of Epstein's imprisonment.

The two men are old friends. They have been ever since Ghislaine Maxwell introduced the prince to her then-beau, sometime in the 1990s. In 2000, Epstein had been invited to Windsor Castle to celebrate the queen's birthday. Six months later, Epstein flew to Sandringham, the queen's estate in Norfolk, England, for a party Prince Andrew threw for Ghislaine's thirty-ninth birthday.

The prince had also visited Epstein on several occasions, in Palm Beach as well as in New York. And if allegations Virginia Roberts made in her 2015 declaration are to be believed, Epstein asked her to give the prince whatever he required, then report back with the details.

According to the *Guardian,* Epstein and the prince had partied together at Windsor Castle, in Saint-Tropez, and in Thailand, where "Andrew was pictured on a yacht surrounded by topless women."

According to Roberts's lawsuit, Epstein had forced her into the prince's bed on Little Saint Jeff's.

* * *

After Epstein's conviction, the British press were using another name for Little Saint Jeff's: Sex Island. The *Guardian* reported that the manager of two Virgin Islands–based corporations owned by Epstein happened to be the wife of the governor of the Virgin Islands. There were allegations involving a million-dollar donation that Epstein had made to the governor's reelection campaign. And then there was Roberts's claim that she had been forced to have sex with the prince on the island as well as in New York and in London.

Invariably, the photograph of Prince Andrew with his arm around the bare midriff of a very young-looking Virginia Roberts ran with stories that appeared in the tabloids.

"It is emphatically denied that the Duke of York had any form of sexual contact or relationship" with Roberts, Buckingham Palace spokespersons would say. "The allegations made are false and without any foundation."

The prince's ex-wife, Sarah Ferguson, the Duchess of York, while on a skiing trip with the prince and their daughter Eugenie in Switzerland, told reporters, "He is the greatest man there is. It was the finest moment of my life in 1986 when I married him. He is a great man, the best in the world."

"I won't stand by—because I know what it feels like to have salacious lies made up about you—and not support him so publicly because they are just shockingly accusatory allegations, which I don't think is right," she said a few days later when interviewed by *Today* host Matt Lauer. "It's a defamation of character, and as a great father and a humongously good man and all the work he does for Britain I won't stand by and let him have his character defamed to this level."

But at the same time, a certain schadenfreude attended the good man's fall from grace, and former associates kept coming out of the woodwork to dish to the press.

"I've seen him treat his staff in a shocking, appalling way," said a former aide to the prince. "He's been incredibly rude to his personal protection officers, literally throwing things on the ground and demanding they 'fucking pick them up.' No social graces at all. Sure, if you're a lady with blond hair and big boobs, then I bet he's utterly charming."

Despite all this, the prince had stuck by Epstein. There was even a photo, frequently trotted out by the tabloids, of the two of them strolling in Central Park.

Some few months before it was taken, a reporter posing as a businessman had secretly taped Sarah Ferguson's demand for five hundred thousand pounds in return for access to the prince.

"If you want to meet him in your business," she'd said then, "look after me, and he'll look after you. You'll get it back tenfold."

"Once again," she said afterward, "my errors have compounded and rebounded and also impacted on the man I admire most in the world: the Duke."

Prince Andrew had had his troubles already—with shady real estate deals, sticky romances, highly embarrassing document dumps (courtesy of Julian Assange and WikiLeaks), and questionable ties to Tunisian oligarchs, corrupt presidents of former Soviet republics, and Mu'ammar Gadhafi, among other entanglements, many of which were explored in a *Vanity Fair* article headlined THE TROUBLE WITH ANDREW.

"The duke has a record of being loyal to his friends," a "royal source" told *Vanity Fair*'s Edward Klein. "Take his feelings for Sarah Ferguson. If you are a prince and you bring a woman into the royal life and, for whatever reasons, she's spit out, you might have feelings of debt toward her. The duke feels that she's been spattered and rejected. His close relationship with the Duchess of York is problematic, and there have been many problems over the last 5 to 10 years, all of which stem from the duchess. Some of the behavior of the duchess is inconsistent with being married to, or an ex-wife of, the duke. There's no question but that Sarah's been a financially self-destructive element in the duke's life."

"The same kind of loyalty manifested itself last December, when the duke visited Epstein at his home in New York," said a spokesperson for Buckingham Palace. "Epstein was a friend of the duke's for the best part of 20 years. It was the first time in four years that he'd seen Epstein. He now recognizes that the meeting in December was unwise."

"Don't expect to see a photo of the two of them together," another "royal source" would say.

But one more story about the prince's dealings with Jeffrey Epstein had already emerged.

At a dinner party at Epstein's town house, the prince dished about the wedding of his nephew Prince William to Kate Middleton.

"He was amused that his dinner companions were so interested in every detail," a guest in attendance told a *New York Post* gossip columnist. "What would Kate wear, what would the Queen wear, would his ex-wife Sarah Ferguson be invited?"

Other guests in attendance that night included Chelsea Handler, George Stephanopoulos, Charlie Rose, Katie Couric, and Woody Allen.

At around the same time, Jeffrey Epstein told the *New York Post,* "I'm not a sexual predator, I'm an 'offender.'

It's the difference between a murderer and a person who steals a bagel."

Was it so remarkable that Prince Andrew would have been seen in Epstein's company? Andrew's philandering had been tabloid fodder for years. Randy Andy, they called him in the UK. And in the circles that Jeffrey Epstein moved in, philandering wasn't seen as a vice. Epstein came of age just as industrywide deregulation took hold on Wall Street. Junk bonds were king. Call girls were charging ten thousand dollars a night. And in the shadows, you'd see things that would have made Caligula blush. Sights that would make Nero himself reach for the nearest fire extinguisher. When the urge presented itself, the new super rich didn't have to swap wives.

They could simply swap harems.

By the same token, was it so very strange to think that a man like the prince would have grown so detached from reality—insofar as *reality* is even a word that applies to a prince? Was it odd that he thought it was absolutely fine to be seen by photographers strolling through Central Park with a registered sex offender—when at the time large swaths of the financial, banking, and trading industries were characterized by their very detachment from day-to-day concerns such as morality, ethics, and appearances?

As for Jeffrey Epstein, one question that might be worth asking is, if he's in fact a narcissist and megalomaniac, could he actually believe that he's *innocent*? Then again, that might be the wrong question. Epstein did plead guilty, after all. But what if he simply doesn't see what he pleaded to as a crime? What if he's *proud* of his lifestyle? And if that's the case, why *wouldn't* Prince

Andrew be proud to be seen in public with his dear friend Jeffrey Epstein?

What if, for people like Epstein and the prince, it's just servants and masters, the way of the world? They're natural winners—*aristocrats,* after all—and if life were fair, well, how would we know who the real winners are?

CHAPTER 59

Anna Salter: November 2015

Why do powerful men do the things that Jeffrey Epstein and Prince Andrew have been accused of doing?

Dr. Anna Salter studies child sex offenders professionally. Educated at Harvard, with a graduate degree in clinical psychology, she spoke, with the benefit of hindsight, about Jeffrey Epstein and others like him from her office in Madison, Wisconsin.

"Consider a car," says Dr. Salter. "There's a motor, and there are brakes. We all have sexual impulses we don't think it would be a good idea to act on. Most of us have good control over our behavior. We have good brakes.

"Sexual offenses and inappropriate sexual behavior are sometimes the result of a bad motor—for example, an attraction to prepubescent children or eleven-to-fourteen-year-old pubescent children as opposed to post-pubescent individuals. But they are always the result of bad brakes.

"Antisocial psychopaths don't have brakes at all."

Dr. Salter has never met Epstein, but she's followed his case closely and finds him a familiar type. She's especially struck by the singular nature of the relationship between powerful, wealthy men and vulnerable, underage women.

"[The men] are more impressive to a fourteen-year-old [girl] than to, say, an adult young woman who is self-supporting and feels more sure of herself," she explains.

"They are attracted to what they call freshness— barely budding sexuality and lack of sexual experience. The difference between them and their victims feeds their ego.

"Great wealth and access are generally factors that make men feel they are entitled to whomever and whatever they want. Some have narcissistic personalities with inflated self-images. And of course, great wealth and status make such men think they can get away with it. Too often, they're right."

On the other hand, Dr. Salter believes that certain conditions, such as the ones exhibited by Jeffrey Epstein, might be an inborn character trait.

Personality can be influenced, sometimes quite heavily, by genetics.

"Virtually no one believes anymore that humans are born a totally blank slate," she explains.

"We arrive with temperamental and personality variations that, of course, the environment can often, but not always, influence. We arrive with baggage."

Is Epstein a born psychopath, then?

"*Psychopathy* is the umbrella term for individuals who do not have a conscience. Pyschopaths are often narcissistic, but narcissists are often not psychopathic. Some individuals who prey on young girls delude themselves into thinking that the abuse will not harm the child. They have a conscience, but they have medicated it with thinking errors. Others are flat-out psychopathic and simply don't care if it hurts the young girl or not. I can't say anything about Epstein, as I have not evaluated him, but narcissism and psychopathy are concepts an evaluator would look at concerning anyone who was sexually attracted to postpubescent individuals but who then began to focus on younger teens.

"Psychopaths are often superficially charming, high-stimulus seekers who are bored if not doing something. They lie, con, and manipulate. They do not establish deep affective ties.

"They are callous and remorseless individuals who simply don't feel bad about harming someone.

"Rules don't apply to them because they are exceptional. They are sure they won't get caught."

CHAPTER 60

Jeffrey Epstein: July 2010

Jeffrey Epstein was done with jail, but he wasn't done settling suits brought by his victims. Under the conditions of his non-prosecution agreement, he's even paid for the victims' lawyers. Still, Epstein's NPA seemed to ensure that he would not be prosecuted again for his crimes. Double jeopardy was working in Epstein's favor. But in July of 2010, reports began to appear in the press: federal investigators were following other leads—leads that could result in child-trafficking charges and a twenty-year sentence.

The Florida attorney general's office refused to comment. It was against policy to confirm or deny the existence of an ongoing investigation. One of Epstein's lawyers told the *Daily Beast* that he had no knowledge of such an investigation. "Jeffrey Epstein has fully complied with all state and federal requirements that arise from the prior proceedings in Palm Beach," Jack Goldberger said. "There are no pending civil lawsuits. There are not and should not be any pending investigations, given Mr.

Epstein's complete fulfillment of all the terms of his non-prosecution agreement with the federal government."

If there was an investigation, nothing had come of it yet. For the moment, Epstein was free—free to turn his attention, again, to intellectual pursuits. He launched a website, JeffreyEpsteinScience.com, that featured blog posts such as "Conversations with Jeffrey Epstein," "The Value of Quantum Computation to Jeffrey Epstein," "Why Evolutionary Biology Intrigues Jeffrey Epstein," and "An Understanding of Theoretical Physics from Jeffrey Epstein." The latter post began: "This is where Jeffrey Epstein takes you to the very cutting edge of the frontiers of knowledge to explore and discuss our basic understanding of the subtle, simple, and hidden [qualities] that lie beneath...our universe."

"Jeffrey doesn't know shit about science," says Stuart Pivar, the art collector who has known Epstein for more than three decades. "Does he like to act like he does? Yes. But he doesn't. But as far as these academic scientists—without people like him they wouldn't have any money."

Other friends of Epstein's say that he truly did have a brilliant mind for science. And in any case, Epstein had done more than sponsor individual scientists. He'd also sponsored conferences on Little Saint Jeff's. On his website, he announced a conference called Mindshift at which Nobel laureates, such as the theoretical physicist Murray Gell-Mann, would mix with surgeons, engineers, and futurists and where professors would discuss cognitive neuroscience, artificial intelligence, systems of encryption and decryption, and other topics.

Epstein had been hosting get-togethers like this for years. Toward the end of Chief Reiter's investigation, in

March of 2006, Epstein had hosted twenty top physicists—including three Nobel Prize winners as well as the celebrity physicist Stephen Hawking—at a Saint Thomas symposium called "Confronting Gravity," which was advertised as "a workshop to explore fundamental questions in physics and cosmology."

"This is a remarkable group," one of the Nobel Prize winners told a reporter for the *St. Thomas Source*.

"There is no agenda except fun and physics, and that's fun with a capital *F*," Epstein said.

Epstein had been especially interested in Stephen Hawking. Someday, Hawking had theorized, the universe would stop expanding and collapse, at which point time would begin to run backwards. Hawking believed that computer viruses were living things. He thought that given the size of the universe, alien life forms existed. He did not believe in God. But he had a vast appreciation for the inner workings of the universe, and this is why Epstein gave Hawking a tremendous gift. He paid to have a submarine modified so that it could fit Hawking and his wheelchair and give the scientist his first glimpse of an actual alien world—the one that lies under the waves of the ocean.

It was one of the most romantic, generous gestures that Jeffrey Epstein had ever made.

CHAPTER 61

Al Seckel: January 2012

Epstein's partner in the Mindshift conference, a man named Al Seckel, was known for throwing fabulous parties that were said to have included the actor Dudley Moore, magician James "the Amazing" Randi, and future Tesla and SpaceX founder Elon Musk, as well as many of the scientists Jeffrey Epstein would court in the course of his own climb up the social ladder.

In certain Los Angeles circles, Al Seckel was a very good man to know. But, like Jeffrey Epstein, Seckel was a sort of illusionist. According to Mark Oppenheimer, a journalist who knew Seckel and followed his career for fifteen years, Seckel made his money by selling rare books and papers, often through his social and academic connections.

"A number of these transactions resulted in accusations and lawsuits," Oppenheimer would write. "In speaking to former Seckel acquaintances, I kept hearing variations on a scheme Mrs. Pearce Williams believed he perpetrated against her late husband, the man Seckel said was his mentor. Seckel took books and promised money, or he took money and promised a book; but somehow, the promised party lost money."

"He was charming, erudite, humorous," one of Seckel's marks told the reporter. "I lent him $75,000. When the time came to pay it back he didn't want to do it."

Oppenheimer found several people whom Seckel had stiffed and uncovered dozens of lawsuits he'd been involved in. In 2007, Seckel settled a libel lawsuit against a man who'd edited his *Wikipedia* page. Years later, Oppenheimer spoke with Seckel's lawyer, Nicholas Hornberger.

"Hornberger confirmed that he'd reached a settlement for the case, a favorable one," the journalist wrote. "Hornberger added that Seckel has still not paid him for his services."

He also interviewed Seckel's wife, Isabel Maxwell.

Al and Isabel met on a blind date and married in Malibu in or "around" 2007 ("I don't keep the dates in my head," Seckel explained). A few years later, they moved to the South of France, where Seckel continued to trade in rare books and papers. While living in France, he was sued by a Virgin Islands company that accused him and Isabel of fraudulently attempting to sell rare books and a seventeenth-century portrait of Isaac Newton.

Seckel had also been trying to sell papers belonging to Isabel's father.

Isabel is Ghislaine Maxwell's sister and the daughter of Robert Maxwell.

It was an odd thing, Epstein's association with this self-professed PhD who, on closer inspection, turned out to be a bit of a grifter. But the Mindshift conference that Epstein and Seckel hosted in the Virgin Islands did take place, in 2010. Murray Gell-Mann was there, along with Leonard Mlodinow, a physicist who coauthored books with Stephen Hawking. Gerald Sussman, an expert on artificial intelligence who taught at MIT and also attended the conference, said that he didn't remember too much about it.

"We had scientific discussions, talked about various things," he said vaguely.

When Mark Oppenheimer asked him if he'd given money to Seckel, Sussman "got testy" with the reporter.

"I have had some dealings with him," Sussman said. "I don't want to say what it's about, because I don't feel good about it, okay?"

Today, Epstein's websites—JeffreyEpsteinFoundation.com and JeffreyEpsteinScience.com—are down. Their domain names have long since expired. Several recipients of Epstein's charitable contributions, including New York's Mount Sinai Hospital and Ballet Palm Beach, announced that they would not be accepting new gifts.

"The further I can keep myself from anything like that the better," said Ballet Palm Beach founder Colleen Smith.

But in 2012, Epstein held one more conference on Little Saint Jeff's. Once again, three Nobel Prize winners were in attendance. Stephen Hawking was also there. All in all, Epstein had gathered twenty-one physicists—from Princeton, Harvard, MIT, and CERN (the European Organization for Nuclear Research)—to "determine what the consensus is, if any, for defining gravity."

According to a press release issued by Epstein's foundation, the consensus that did emerge was that space is "not quite empty."

CHAPTER 62

Jeffrey Epstein: February 2, 2011

It's Groundhog Day, and once-reclusive Jeffrey Epstein is hitting the peak of his fame in a ripped-from-the-headlines episode of *Law & Order: SVU* that tracks, eerily well, with his own legal history.

The setup for this episode is the rape of a very young French girl. One who's been flown to New York on a very rich man's private jet, then flown back—coach class—to Paris.

On the plane, she has a freak-out. She thinks the middle-aged guy sitting next to her is trying to rape her. In Paris, the local police get involved.

"It was just a birthday party," the tearful girl tells the SVU cops via videoconference from France. "We were his present."

The cops ask: Whose present?

"The billionaire. The one who owns the jet."

Does the French girl know his name?

"Jordan. He wanted a massage. But I had to take off my clothes. He climbed on top of me. It hurt. I started to bleed, and it wouldn't stop. The doctor came."

"Dominique," the cops say. "We're going to arrest this man. But we need you to return to New York so you can testify."

"Non," says the girl. *"Non! Jamais! Jamais!"*

For Epstein, there are other embarrassments, many of which have to do with his royal friends. The wedding of Prince William and Kate Middleton is approaching, and the ongoing troubles of Prince William's uncle Prince Andrew keep threatening to derail the festivities. On March 6, a spokesperson for Sarah Ferguson confirms that Epstein paid off part of the seventy-eight thousand pounds that the duchess borrowed from a man who was once her personal assistant.

The next day, headlines appear in the *Telegraph* and other British papers: DUKE OF YORK "APPEALED TO JEFFREY EPSTEIN TO HELP DUCHESS PAY DEBT."

"I personally, on behalf of myself, deeply regret that Jeffrey Epstein became involved in any way with me," Prince Andrew's ex-wife tells journalists. "I abhor paedophilia and any sexual abuse of children and know that this was a gigantic error of judgment on my behalf.

"I am just so contrite I cannot say. Whenever I can I will repay the money and will have nothing ever to do with Jeffrey Epstein ever again."

That week, as part of the ongoing civil lawsuits against Epstein, Sarah Kellen and Nadia Marcinkova are both asked about Prince Andrew's relations with Epstein.

"Would you agree with me that Prince Andrew and Jeffrey Epstein used to share underaged girls for sexual relations?" Kellen is asked.

"On the instructions of my lawyer," Kellen replies, "I must invoke my Fifth Amendment privilege."

"Have you ever been made to perform sexually on Prince Andrew?" lawyers ask Marcinkova.

"Fifth" is Nadia's simple, succinct reply.

That same week, the government downgrades Prince Andrew's role as Great Britain's royal trade envoy. But the British press is tenacious, and in the *Telegraph,* the *Guardian,* and elsewhere, stories appear on a daily basis:

- *The Duke, His Paedophile Guest, and the Most Unusual Use of an RAF Base*
- *Andrew's Secret Love Life Revealed*
- *Royal Connections: Prince Andrew and the Paedophile Are Suddenly the Talk of New York*
- *Time to Show This Right Royal Clown the Door*
- *An Odd Trio: The Royal Trade Envoy, the Teenage Masseuse and the Fixer*
- *No. 10 Struggles to Contain Row Over Prince*
- *From Royal Asset to National Liability*
- *Royal Blush*
- *Duke Could Be Called to Two Epstein Trials*
- *It's the Company You Keep… The Duke's Dangerous Liaisons*
- *Nothing Grand About This Old Duke of York*
- *The Royal Family Has Feared a Blow-Up Over Duke's Choice of Friends For Years*
- *Our Less-Than-Grand Old Duke of York*

On March 11, a devastating undersea earthquake and tsunami move Japan's main island by several feet, shifting the earth on its axis. The destruction is horrific and unprecedented. But on March 13, the *Daily Mail* devotes four pages and seven separate articles to Prince Andrew. That same day, the *Telegraph* runs three pieces, and the

Sunday Times runs a two-page spread headlined GUN SMUGGLER BOASTS OF SWAY OVER ANDREW.

On March 14, the *Guardian* runs one more piece about Andrew's troubles.

PRINCE ANDREW DOMINATES HEADLINES DESPITE THE EARTHQUAKE, the headline reads.

CHAPTER 63

Alan Dershowitz: September 2014

If the ongoing lawsuits are costing Epstein millions, he has millions left to spare. Meanwhile, the FBI's investigation into whether Epstein trafficked underage women across state lines seems to be going nowhere. As 2014 draws to a close, it's beginning to look as if Epstein is finally free and clear of the case.

But for Epstein's friend and sometime lawyer Alan Dershowitz, things are about to get very unpleasant.

At the start of 2008, Bradley Edwards, the Fort Lauderdale lawyer, had filed a motion in a West Palm Beach court on behalf of two unnamed women accusing Prince Andrew and Alan Dershowitz of participating directly in Epstein's illegal activities.

Prince Andrew had had no comment to make, and Dershowitz had objected to the accusations in the strongest possible terms.

"There's absolutely no kernel of truth to this story," he'd said. "I don't know this woman. I've never been in the same place with her. She's made the whole story up out of whole cloth."

Bradley Edwards had already become involved in lawsuits against Epstein. In 2007, working with a former federal judge and University of Utah law professor named Paul Cassell, he had filed a lawsuit on behalf of another unnamed woman. Six years later, that case is still pending, and now, Edwards and Cassell petition to have the two suits combined.

All in all, four Jane Does take part in the lawsuit.

Jane Doe 3 is Virginia Roberts, the girl who says that Ghislaine Maxwell recruited her for Epstein at Trump's resort, Mar-a-Lago.

Epstein had "lent" her and other young girls to prominent businessmen, important politicians, world leaders, and other powerful men in order "to ingratiate himself with them for business, personal, political, and financial gain, as well as to obtain blackmail information," Roberts claims.

She says that Epstein forced her and other underage girls to take part in an orgy in the Virgin Islands.

She names Prince Andrew and Alan Dershowitz as two of the men she'd been forced to have sex with and claims that Dershowitz had been "an eyewitness to the sexual abuse of many other minors by Epstein and several of Epstein's co-conspirators."

This time, Prince Andrew does respond to the allegations.

"This relates to longstanding and ongoing civil proceedings in the United States, to which the Duke of York is not a party," Buckingham Palace says in a short statement. "As such we would not comment on the detail. However, for the avoidance of doubt, any suggestion of impropriety with underage minors is categorically untrue."

Alan Dershowitz also goes on the attack. Virginia's claims are part of a plot to extort him, he claims. The motion that Edwards and Cassell have filed is "the sleaziest legal document" he's ever seen.

"They manipulated a young, suggestible woman who was interested in money," Dershowitz says. "This is a disbarrable offense, and they will be disbarred. They will rue the day they ever made this false charge against me." It's a vehement denial. But then, the allegations made by Virginia Roberts, on January 15, 2015, in a declaration filed against the government in an attempt to overturn Jeffrey Epstein's non-prosecution agreement, are highly disturbing.

CHAPTER 64

Declaration of Virginia Roberts Giuffre, filed on January 19, 2015 by attorneys representing Jeffrey Epstein's victims (continued)

20. Harvard law professor Alan Dershowitz was around Epstein frequently. Dershowitz was so comfortable with the sex [that] was going on that on one occasion he observed me in sexual activity with Epstein.

21. I had sexual intercourse with Dershowitz at least six times. The first time was when I was about 16, early on in my servitude to Epstein, and it continued until I was 19.

22. The first time we had sex took place in New York in Epstein's home. It was in Epstein's room (not the massage room). I was approximately sixteen years old at the time. I called Dershowitz "Alan." I knew he was a famous professor.

23. The second time that I had sex with Dershowitz was at Epstein's house in Palm Beach.

24. I also had sex with Dershowitz at Epstein's Zorro Ranch in New Mexico in the massage room off of the indoor pool area, which was still being painted.

25. We also had sex at Little Saint James Island in the U.S. Virgin Islands.

26. Another sexual encounter between me and Dershowitz happened on Epstein's airplane. Another girl was present on the plane with us.

27. I have recently seen Alan Dershowitz on television calling me a "liar." He is lying by denying that he had sex with me. The man I've seen on television, described as a former law professor, is the same man that I had sex with at least six times. Dershowitz also knows that Epstein had sex with other underage girls and lent me out to other people, but he is lying and denying that. . . .

28. After years of abuse and being lent out, I began to look for a way to escape. I had first gone into Epstein's household because I wanted to be a massage therapist. Epstein had taken me into his clutches through promises and talk and for some time I believed him. But once he had me under his control, regardless of my doubts and fears, I felt trapped.

29. I kept asking Epstein for my promised training and education. Epstein finally got me a plane ticket to Thailand to go to Chiang Mai to learn Thai massage. This sounded like my chance to escape. In September 2002, I packed my bags for good. I knew this would be my only opportunity to break away.

30. On September 27, 2002, I flew from JFK in New York to Chiang Mai, Thailand. I arrived around September 29 for my training. But Epstein was going to get something out of this trip as well. I was supposed to interview a girl and bring her back to the United States for Epstein.

31. [Left blank in the original]

32. I did the massage training in Chiang Mai. While I was there, I met a great and special guy and

told him honestly what I was being forced to do. He told me I should get out of it. I told him that the people I was working for were very powerful and that I could not walk away or disobey them without risking serious punishment, including my life. He told me he would protect me. I had confidence [in] him and I saw his love and help as my opportunity to escape and to be with someone who truly loved me and would protect me. I married him and flew to Australia.

33. I called Epstein and told him I was not coming back. He asked why? I said "I've fallen in love." Epstein basically said "good luck and have a good life." I could tell he was not happy. I was afraid of what he was going to do to me. I thought he or one of his powerful friends might send someone to hurt me or have me killed.

34. From that point onward, out of concern for my safety and general well-being, I stayed in Australia with my husband. I was in Australia from late 2002 to October 2013. To be clear, I was never in the United States during these years, not even for a short trip to visit my mother. And my absence from the United States was not voluntary—I was hiding from Epstein out of fear of what he would do to me if I returned to the United States.

35. In around 2007, after not hearing from anyone for years, out of the blue I was contacted by someone who identified himself with a plain sounding name and claimed he was with the FBI. It seemed very odd for someone doing an official criminal investigation to just call up on the phone like that. I hadn't heard Epstein's name for years. I didn't know who this person was and what it was really about. I couldn't tell what was going on.

36. This man said he was looking into Jeffrey Epstein. The man asked if I had been involved with Epstein. My first instinct was to say nothing because I wasn't sure he was really with the FBI or any authorities. I answered a few basic questions, telling him that I knew Jeffrey Epstein and had met him at a young age. But the conversation didn't feel right. This man never offered to come and meet with me in person. Instead, he asked me right off the bat about Epstein's sexual practices. I thought it would be strange for a true law enforcement officer to behave that way, so I became increasingly uncomfortable and suspicious about who was actually calling me.

37. I told the man nothing more about Epstein. The conversation probably didn't even last three minutes, but it immediately triggered all of the fears of Epstein and his powerful friends that had caused me to escape in the first place. If the call accomplished anything, it only put me back in a state of fear and told me that I could be found quite easily and had nobody officially protecting me.

38. I suspected that the man who called me was working for Epstein or one of Epstein's powerful friends. I believed that if this was really an agent who was investigating Epstein, he would have known who I was and how I fit into Epstein's sexual crimes in many different places. He would have interviewed me in a way that would have established his credentials and would have shown how he could provide potential protection from Epstein. That never happened.

39. Getting a call from this supposed FBI agent made me scared all over again. I had left the old life of sexual slavery behind me and started a new life in a new country in hopes that the powerful people whose illegal activities I knew all about would never find me.

40. *Shortly after this purported FBI call, I was con-tacted by telephone by someone who appeared clearly to be working for Epstein. The caller told me about an investigation into Epstein and said that some of the girls being questioned were saying that Epstein had had sexual contact with them. After they made these allegations, the man said they were being discred-ited as drug addicts and prostitutes, but in my case, if I were to keep quiet, I would "be looked after." The fact that this call was made shortly after the supposed FBI call reinfor[c]ed my concern that the man I had talked to earlier was not really working for the FBI but for Epstein. I didn't think that the FBI and Epstein would both be working together and would both get my phone number at almost exactly the same time. I played along and told this person that I had gotten a call from the "FBI" but that I didn't tell him anything. The person on the phone was pleased to hear [that].*

41. *A short time later, one of Epstein's lawyers (not Alan Dershowitz) called me, and then got Epstein on the line at the same time. Epstein and his lawyer basically asked again if I was going to say anything. The clear implication was that I should not. The way they were talking to me, I was afraid of what would happen if I didn't keep quiet. My thought was that if I didn't say what they wanted me to say, or not to say, I might get hurt.*

42. *I promised Epstein and his lawyer that I would keep quiet. They seemed happy with that and that seemed to me to [be the] way to keep me and my fam-ily safe. And I did what Epstein and his lawyer told me. I kept quiet.*

This declaration, stricken from the record by the judge in the victims' lawsuit against the government, also set in motion events that led to Dershowitz's and Roberts's lawyers becoming involved in spectacular lawsuits, which included a complaint by Dershowitz that these allegations were false and had defamed him, and a complaint by Edwards that Dershowitz's accusations against him were false and defamatory.

CHAPTER 65

Alan Dershowitz: October 2015

About fifteen minutes into the ripped-from-the-headlines episode of *Law & Order: SVU* that was inspired by the Jeffrey Epstein saga, the plot takes an interesting turn: before officers have a chance to arrest him, Jordan, the character modeled on Epstein, shows up at SVU headquarters.

The twelve-year-old French girl raped *him,* Jordan says.

Wearing a monogrammed fleece pullover like the ones favored by Jeffrey Epstein, he describes an evening at home.

"The party was in full swing," he explains. "A friend said she wanted to give me a *special* present. Told me to wait in my massage room—"

An SVU guy interrupts: "Guy has a massage room?"

"I suffer from chronic back pain," Jordan says.

"While I was waiting, I fell asleep. Now, at first I thought I must be dreaming. I was aroused. I felt myself being manually manipulated. Then I remembered it was my present. I started to enjoy myself. But then it got rough, and that's when I opened my eyes."

"What did you see?"

"A woman. A woman I'd never seen before."

"A woman? Dominique Moreau was *twelve!*"

"It was dark. I just wanted her off of me. I tried to stop her."

"But the twelve-year-old overpowered you?"

"No. She *threatened* me. She said if I didn't let her ... continue, she was going to scream 'Rape.'"

"And there was nothing that you could do? You've got forty years and a hundred pounds on the girl."

"The party was going on right outside the door. I knew how this was going to look. I was naked. She was naked. What could I do?"

It was a brilliant plot twist—one that ultimately allowed Jordan to get off scot-free.

But the plot twist that Epstein's own story ended up taking on the day of Alan Dershowitz's deposition at a Broward County, Florida, courthouse was even more surprising.

"There was a criminal extortion plot," Alan Dershowitz told Brad Edwards and Paul Cassell's lawyer, Jack Scarola, on October 15, 2015.

"Your clients were involved."

Bradley and Cassell had sued Dershowitz in Broward County for defamation—payback for extremely negative comments the law professor had made in the media.

Dershowitz had countersued. His reputation was on the line, and he had come armed for battle.

"I'm thrilled they sued me," he'd told reporters. "In the end, someone will be disbarred. Either it will be me or the two lawyers."

But if Dershowitz was swinging for the fences in his struggle to keep his hard-earned reputation afloat, he still had a bombshell to drop. When deposed by Scarola, he proposed his own theory about why Virginia Roberts had named him, along with Prince Andrew, as one of the men who had sexually abused her at Epstein's New Mexico ranch, in New York City, and in Palm Beach.

A theory that implicated the lawyers who were suing *him* in a much larger conspiracy.

According to Dershowitz, Brad Edwards pressured Virginia Roberts into identifying Dershowitz as one her assailants.

Dershowitz said that Edwards did this so that they could blackmail Jeffrey Epstein's patron Leslie Wexner for one *billion* dollars.

Roberts lied about him, Dershowitz maintained, to give Wexner an idea of what would happen to him if Edwards's demands weren't met.

Furthermore, Dershowitz said, he had *proof*.

CHAPTER 66

Excerpts from the Deposition of Alan Dershowitz: October 15, 2015

9:46 a.m.

Q: In an interview with Hala Gorani on January 5 of this year, broadcast on *CNN Live,* you said, "I have a superb memory." Do you acknowledge having made that statement?

A: I have a superb memory, so I must have made that statement. My mother had an extraordinary memory, and when I was in college and I was on the debate team, my mother allowed me to debate on the Sabbath, which was Jewish rest day, only on the condition that I not take notes or write. And at that point I discovered that I have a very good memory and don't have to—generally didn't have to take notes. My memory, obviously, at the age of seventy-seven has slipped a bit; but do I have a very good memory, yes.

* * *

10:18 a.m.

Q: Which of my clients are you swearing under oath encouraged Virginia Roberts to include allegations of an encounter with you at the New Mexico ranch?

A: Both of them—both of your clients, both Judge Cassell and Mr. Edwards—were both involved in encouraging [their] client to file a perjurious affidavit that they knew or should have known was perjurious recently when they sought to file another defamatory allegation in the federal proceeding.

Q: Was the arrangement such that what you are charging Bradley Edwards and Professor Paul Cassell with doing was suborning perjury?

A: Absolutely. If you ask me the question, I am directly charging Judge Cassell and Bradley Edwards with suborning perjury. I have been advised that Virginia Roberts did not want to mention me, told her friends that she did not want to mention me. And was, quote, pressured by her lawyers into including these totally false allegations against me. Yes, your clients are guilty of suborning perjury.

Q: Who told you that Bradley Edwards pressured Virginia Roberts into falsely identifying you?

A: A friend of Virginia Roberts who called me out of the blue and told me that she was horrified by what was happening to me and that she recently had meetings with Virginia Roberts and Virginia Roberts had told her that she never mentioned me previously. That the lawyers pressured her into mentioning me. And mentioning me over her desire not to mention me, yes.

10:20 a.m.

Q: What was the name of the person?

A: Her name is—her first name is Rebecca.

Q: Yes.

A: I don't know the last name.

Q: Did you attempt to find out her last name?

A: I have her last name written down, but—

Q: Where?

A: It's in my—in my notes. And I could get it for you....

Q: When did you write Rebecca's name down?

A: When she—when she first called me—let me be very clear, since you've asked me the question.

At first her husband and she called me on the phone. They would not give me their names. But they told me [the] story. We had a series of phone conversations in which I asked them, please, to tell me their names. And after a period of time, after they told me the story in great detail, she was willing to give me her name. She asked me to promise that I would not disclose her identity without her permission. I have been trying to call her. Called her as recently as this morning and last night.

I want to recall—I don't think I called her this morning. I called her twice last night to try to get her permission to reveal her complete name and identity. But I have the name, and I will be happy to give it to you. I just don't have it off the top of my head.

* * *

10:23 a.m.

Q: Would you tell us how many phone conversations
    [you had] with this person Rebecca?
A: More than six. Probably between six and ten, maybe
    closer to ten. The first few [times] she called me, and
    after I got their number I called her a number of
    times.
Q: What is her husband's name?
A: Michael. Different last name from hers, but again.
Q: Where do they live?
A: Palm Beach. Or West Palm Beach, in the Palm
    Beach area. They have been friends of Virginia
    Roberts since she was a young child.
Q: Were there any witnesses to any of these phone
    conversations other than Rebecca, Michael, and
    you?
A: Yes.
Q: Who?
A: My wife.
Q: When did the first conversation occur?
A: I can probably get you specific information about
    that. But it was months ago. When the story was
    in the newspapers, she called and related the entire
    story to me and related to me that it was part of a
    massive extortion plot.

10:25 a.m.

Q: Did you take contemporaneous notes of those phone
    conversations?

A: No. I took note of names, but not really notes of the substance, no.

Q: Have you ever made notes with regard to the substance of any communications that you allegedly had with Rebecca and/or Michael?

A: I didn't "allegedly" have these conversations. I had these conversations. And I don't recall taking notes of those conversations.

10:44 a.m.

Q: How many phone calls did you have with this person Rebecca before she informed you as to the reason why she was calling you?

A: She informed me the first time.

Q: The very first conversation.

A: Yes.

Q: How many phone calls was it before she asked you for money?

A: She never asked me for money.

Q: How many phone calls was it before her husband asked you for money?

A: I was never asked for money, ever.

Q: Do you know how it is that these people knew how to contact you?

A: They told me they went to my website and got my number and left a message for me to call. Yeah, that's what happened. Oh, no; they sent me—they went on my website and sent me an e-mail and asked me—and the e-mail had a blank name but a way to respond. And so I responded with my phone number and they called, is my recollection. That's my best recollection.

* * *

10:45 a.m.

Q: So from the very first conversation that you had with this person, you had information indicating that this person was informing you that Bradley Edwards had engaged in unethical conduct, correct?

A: Let me just be very clear what she said to me. She said to me that she had been told directly by her friend Virginia Roberts, who stayed with her overnight for a period of time, that she never wanted to mention me in any of the pleadings. And that her two lawyers in the pleadings, or her lawyers who filed the pleadings, pressured her into including my name and details.

Q: Did Rebecca ever suggest to you that the details sworn to by Virginia Roberts were false?

A: She certainly suggested that, yes. She mentioned to me that Virginia Roberts had never, ever mentioned [me to her], among any of the people that she had had any contact with, until she—until she was pressured into doing so by her lawyers, yes.

Q: So from the very first conversation, the impression you had was that this was a witness who could provide information that Bradley Edwards and Paul Cassell had acted unethically and dishonestly, correct?

A: I wasn't sure she could provide the information because she was very reluctant to come forward. She didn't want to be involved. But I knew she had provided me with information, yes, but I didn't know, and I still don't know, whether she is prepared to be a witness. I don't know the answer to that question.

* * *

11:08 a.m.

Q: Was any request made by you for a meeting?

A: Yes.

Q: Let me back up then, if I could, please. Because what I want you to do, based upon your superb memory, is to tell us in as much detail as you possibly can recall everything that was said....

A: I'm not sure the request for the meeting came in the first call or the second call.... The first call was basically, I'd really like to talk to your wife [Rebecca] about this. I'm happy to fly down. I'm happy to talk to you on the phone. And we left it that they would think—that she would—that he would ask her to think about it. And that I could call back in a—in a few days and find out what her—what her current feelings were.

Q: Where were you when you received this phone call—or when you made this phone call? Sorry.

A: I think I was in New York.

Q: Do you know whether that phone call was made on a cell phone or a landline?

A: I don't remember.

Q: Have you attempted to gather your telephone records for purposes of responding to discovery requests in this case?

A: I left that to my lawyers. I know that we did produce telephone records during the relevant periods of time when Virginia Roberts knew Jeffrey Epstein, and those telephone records established that I could not have been at the locations and at the times that Virginia Roberts claimed to have had—falsely claimed to have [had] sexual contact with me.

Q: I promise you we're going to get to those.

A: Good.

Q: Promise you. Along with all the flight logs that you claim exonerate you.

11:11 a.m.

Q: Let's go to the very second contact that you had with either Michael or Rebecca. Who initiated the second contact?

A: I think I did. I called and got Michael on the phone.

Q: Where did you call from?

A: I think New York.

Q: Tell me in as much detail as your superb memory allows you to recall everything that was said during the course of that phone conversation.

[Dershowitz's lawyer]: Let's object to the form and the continued use of the word *superb*. He's described his memory. That's your characterization. Go ahead.

Q: No, I think that that was Mr. Dershowitz's characterization, which I have adopted.

[Lawyer]: Okay. Go ahead.

A: I called, spoke to Michael. I asked Michael if he had spoken to his wife. She said yes, and she was still reluctant to talk to me.

Q: I'm sorry—she said yes when you asked Michael if he had spoken to his wife?

A: He said yes. And that she was still reluctant to talk to me. I suggested to him that perhaps she could talk to me briefly just so that she hears what I have to say. And he could listen and remain on the phone, and she could stop at any time she wanted. And there came a time during that conversation when she did get on the phone, and here's what she told me. She said she had grown up with Virginia Roberts. That they were very, very close friends as young people. That Virginia Roberts came to stay with her for a number of days, I think it was over Halloween, and they had gone out and had dinner, just the two of them. And that she confided in her; Virginia Roberts confided in Rebecca that she had never wanted to mention me in any of the pleadings, but she was pressured by her lawyer into doing so. Rebecca then said that I was not the object of this effort. The object of the effort was a billionaire who lives in Columbus, Ohio, and who owns Victoria's Secret and Limited Too. Rebecca told me she did not know the name of that billionaire, but that Virginia and her lawyers hoped to get one billion dollars, b-i-l-l-i-o-n, one billion dollars, or half of his net worth, from him by alleging that he had improperly engaged in sexual misconduct with Virginia Roberts. That money would be divided three ways: a third of it to Virginia Roberts, a third of it to a charity that she and her lawyers were setting up for battered women, and a third of it to the lawyers.

She then told me that they were trying to get ABC News to interview Virginia Roberts so as to give her credibility in order to pressure the billionaire from Columbus, Ohio, into paying a large sum of money. And that I was named as an effort to try to show the billionaire what could happen to somebody if they were accused of sexual misconduct. And that would encourage him to settle a lawsuit or pay money in exchange for his name not being mentioned or revealed. I had no idea about this. And I didn't—I didn't ask about this. She just stated this. And I then corroborated the fact that she was absolutely correct in everything she had said to me.

Q: You corroborated the fact that she was absolutely correct in everything that she had said to you?

A: That's right.

Q: How?

A: Okay. Let me answer that question. I was very—I wasn't sure, so I called Leslie Wexner. I got his wife on the phone, Abigail Wexner. Obviously I knew that the only billionaire in Columbus, Ohio, who owned Limited Too and who owned Victoria's Secret was Leslie Wexner. I had met Leslie Wexner on two occasions, I think, and his wife. I called Abigail on the phone and I said, "I think you ought to know that there is an extortion plot being directed against your husband by unscrupulous lawyers in— in Florida." And she said, "Oh, we're aware of that; they've already been in contact with us," which surprised me. But [her statement] was confirmation of that. I then also—I can't give you the chronology of that. I then was in touch with ABC and found out she was absolutely correct about her efforts to try to get interviewed on ABC television. In fact, I learned that your client, Brad Edwards, had sent a communication to people in the area urging them to watch her interview that was scheduled to be on three television programs. If I'm not mistaken, it was [the] *Good Day Show,* the evening news, and the show *Nightline....* I then was in communication with ABC and helped to persuade them that they would be putting false information on the air if they allowed Virginia Roberts to tell her false story. So I was able to corroborate that. I then also corroborated the fact that she had never mentioned me when her boyfriend appeared on television and publicly stated that she had never mentioned me in any of her description[s] of people who she had sexual contact with. So I was then completely satisfied that Rebecca was telling me the complete truth. And that in my view, there was an extortion plot directed against Leslie Wexner, a criminal extortion plot directed against Leslie Wexner, and that your clients were involved in that extortion plot.

11:30 a.m.

Q: Let's see if we can make sure that we're understanding one another, sir. Do you recognize that there's a distinction between Virginia Roberts having met you, having been sexually abused by you on multiple occasions, but not wanting to name you as opposed to Virginia Roberts never having met you and never having been sexually abused by you...? Are those two things different in your mind?

A: Not in the context of this case. Because Virginia Roberts said that she was going to seek justice from everybody that had abused her. And if she didn't want to name me, I think the inference is inescapable that I was not among those people that she had had any sexual contact with. So that was certainly the inference I drew....

11:35 a.m.

Q: Who are the people that Rebecca says Virginia had previously told her that Virginia was abused by?

A: I never asked her that question.

Q: Did you ask her was Les Wexner one of the people that abused Virginia?

A: I told you I never asked her the question.

Q: Are you aware that years before December of 2014, when the CVRA pleading was filed, that your name had come up repeatedly in connection with Jeffrey Epstein's abuse of minors, correct?

A: I am aware that never before 2014, end of December, was it ever, ever alleged that I had acted in any way inappropriately with regard to Virginia Roberts, that I ever touched her, that I ever met her, that I had ever been with her. I was completely aware of that. There had never been any allegation. She claims under oath that she told you that secretly in 2011, but you have produced no notes of any such conversation. You, of course, are a witness to this allegation and will be deposed as a witness to this allegation. I believe it is an entirely false allegation that she told you in 2011 that she had had any sexual contact with me. I think she's lying through her teeth when she says that. And I doubt that your notes will reveal any such information. But if she did tell you that, she would be absolutely, categorically lying. So I am completely aware that never—until the lies were put in a legal pleading at the end of December 2014, it was never alleged that I had any sexual contact with Virginia Roberts. I know that it was alleged that I was a witness to Jeffrey Epstein's alleged abuse, and that was false. I was never a witness to any of Jeffrey Epstein's sexual abuse. And I wrote that to you, something that you have falsely denied. And I stand on the record. The record is clear that I have categorically denied I was ever a witness to any abuse, that I ever saw Jeffrey Epstein abusing anybody. And—and the very idea that I would stand and talk to Jeffrey Epstein while he was receiving oral sex from Virginia Roberts, which she swore to under oath, is so outrageous, so preposterous, that even

David Boies [a prominent lawyer associated with the firm representing Virginia Roberts] said he couldn't believe it was true.

12:24 p.m.

Q: You engaged in a mass-media campaign to convince the world that Bradley Edwards and Professor Paul Cassell were unethical lawyers who had fabricated false charges against you, correct?

A: No, that's not correct. I responded to press inquiries by telling the truth. My goal was to let the world know that Virginia Roberts's allegations against me were totally false. These two stories appeared, as far as I can tell, in every single newspaper in the world and on every media, which was part of their plot and the plan of your clients, which is why they absurdly mentioned Prince Andrew, claiming in the most absurd way—that they mentioned him because he was trying to lobby prosecutors to get a reduced sentence for Jeffrey Epstein; they obviously put Prince Andrew in there in order to get massive publicity around the world. And every media in the world, practically, called me, from the BBC to CBS to ABC to CNN, and I responded to lies with the truth.

Q: And the truth that you attempted to convey was that Bradley Edwards and Professor Paul Cassell were unethical lawyers who fabricated false charges against you, right?

A: The truth that I intended to convey was that the charges against me were false and fabricated, that I never had any sexual contact—

Q: Fabricated by whom, sir?

A: Please don't interrupt me.... that I never had any sexual contact with Virginia Roberts. Because Professor Cassell insisted on conveying to the public that he was a former judge and that he was a professor and that he was using—improperly, in my view—the stationery and name of his university to add credibility to his claims, I felt that it was imperative for me to indicate that he was engaging in improper and unethical conduct. It would have been improper for me to have allowed his use of his credibility as a former federal judge, as a professor who uses, misuses, his university imprimatur—it was very important for me to attack the credibility of the messengers of the false information. And it was important for me to also remind the public that Bradley Edwards was a partner of [Scott] Rothstein, a man who is spending fifty years in jail for fraudulently creating a Ponzi scheme to sell Jeffrey Epstein cases that didn't exist.

CHAPTER 67

Scott Rothstein: 2009

Scott Rothstein was a flashy Fort Lauderdale ex-lawyer who parked his collection of cars in an air-conditioned warehouse, kept a copy of the Torah on his desk, and hung a portrait of Al Pacino as Michael Corleone outside his office. One of his nicknames was TPOFD, short for "the Prince of Fucking Darkness," and in private, he'd say things like: "Understand that the repercussions of engaging me could open the gates of hell. Understand that I am capable of evil far beyond anything your imagination could ever conjure up."

Rothstein hosted receptions for prominent politicians—John McCain, Bobby Jindal, Arnold Schwarzenegger—and handed out hundreds of thousands of dollars at a time in campaign contributions. He gave millions more to charitable institutions: the Joe DiMaggio Children's Hospital; the American Heart Association. By all outward appearances, he could afford it: seventy lawyers worked in his firm, which had offices in Florida, New York, and Venezuela. But Rothstein's millions actually came from a $1.2 billion Ponzi scheme he'd been running since 2005.

In April of 2009, Bradley Edwards joined Rothstein's firm. The lawyer brought his papers along, and Rothstein showed those pertaining to Epstein to potential investors. In exchange for a lump sum up front, Rothstein said, investors would receive a far larger chunk of money later, which Epstein would pay in future settlements.

Edwards and Rothstein both say that Edwards had no knowledge whatsoever of the Ponzi scheme. (Prosecutors, and the Florida Bar, agree.) Edwards left as soon as he caught wind of the scheme, in November of 2009. But the few months he spent in Rothstein's company gave Dershowitz the opening he needed to pry open Virginia Roberts's accusations.

It was at Edwards's insistence, Dershowitz would say, as well as Paul Cassell's, that Virginia Roberts added Dershowitz's name to the list of men she claimed had abused her.

According to Dershowitz, he'd been pulled into a billion-dollar extortion plot Edwards had hatched. And for Edwards and Cassell, there had been a secondary benefit: Dershowitz had helped to work out Epstein's confidential non-prosecution agreement with the government. By implicating him directly in Epstein's abuse of underage women, Dershowitz claimed, Edwards and Cassell were trying to "open up" that agreement.

It might have been a Hail Mary pass on the part of Alan Dershowitz.

But the argument had its own internal logic.

The idea that Bradley Edwards and Paul Cassell were trying to blackmail *Leslie Wexner*—blackmail him for one *billion* dollars, no less—sounds highly improbable. But we do know for a fact that Edwards had worked with Rothstein—a man who'd been running his own billion-dollar con.

Edwards may not have known that Rothstein was taking his files on Jeffrey Epstein and showing them to investors. But Edwards's *proximity* to Rothstein didn't look good. It may not have been as damaging as Dershowitz's close friendship with Epstein, but it was damaging nonetheless. It gave Dershowitz the opening he needed to make his argument. And the genius of Dershowitz's argument was that it wasn't necessarily predicated on an actual plot to blackmail Wexner. Maybe the thing Edwards was really after was the idea that *a lawyer who helped work out Epstein's non-prosecution agreement* was also having sex with Virginia Roberts. That *would* give Edwards leverage in trying to crack the agreement open. And in that case, was it so hard to imagine him pressuring Virginia Roberts to add Dershowitz's name to the list?

Perhaps it wasn't, in this scenario. Virginia would have still felt reluctant to mention Dershowitz. If she was, there was the matter of the three hundred million dollars, and then some, that she would stand to gain. And the three hundred million or so that goes to set up a charity for battered women? If the scenario Dershowitz had thrown out was true, that would have been a genius move on Edwards's part—the sort of detail that helps the whole psychological picture fall into place. If Virginia felt guilty for lying about Dershowitz, she could think of the thousands of battered women she'd end up helping.

All these possibilities seemed bizarre. And yet *everything* connected with Epstein's story seemed to be bizarre.

Bill Clinton got the use of a jet out of Epstein—a trip to Africa. But he and Epstein weren't bosom buddies.

As for Prince Andrew, we already know how he feels about women.

But what did Dershowitz get out of Epstein, aside from Epstein's wise counsel on all the books he'd written?

One advantage Dershowitz had, as he laid out his argument, was that when it came to Jeffrey Epstein, all bets were off. He didn't have to establish his innocence. All he had to do was make sure that the waters stayed muddy. The more complicated things seemed to be, the better they were for Dershowitz.

Thanks to Jeffrey Epstein's actions, and the endlessly complicated cycle of suits and countersuits those actions inspired, those waters were very muddy indeed.

CODA

Scott Rothstein

On October 27, 2009, Florida's governor, Charlie Crist, left Scott Rothstein a voice-mail message.

"Hey, Scott," the governor said. "It's Charlie, your favorite Greek governor. Hope you're doing well, buddy. Just wanted to touch base and let you know I'm working Versace for November twenty-fourth, and it is going amazingly well—unbelievable, brother.... Really enjoyed again seeing you and Kimmie and watch[ing] a little football and best to you guys from Carol and me. We love you. Take care. Bye-bye."

That same day, Rothstein took a chartered Gulf-stream V to Casablanca, Morocco. For a while, it seemed as if Rothstein was running. But a few days later, the same Gulfstream returned to Fort Lauderdale. The Ponzi king had decided to turn himself in.

The moment he did, he started to sing like a canary in return for a lenient sentence. Rothstein gave up dozens of associates—the list included people at his law firm, law enforcement officers, and his own wife, Kimmie, who was arrested for hiding more than one million dollars' worth of jewelry.

All in all, more than thirty people involved in Rothstein's schemes were arrested and sentenced.

Thanks, in part, to his cooperation with the feds, his was the only Ponzi scheme in history in which all the victims recovered their money. In return, Rothstein was put into a witness protection program and is serving his fifty-year sentence anonymously, in an undisclosed prison location.

Alan Dershowitz

On November 10, 2015, Alan Dershowitz arrived at Shriver Hall, on the campus of Johns Hopkins University, in Baltimore, to talk about the Arab-Israeli conflict.

"The outlines for peace are so obvious," he said. "There has to be a two-state solution."

Fifteen minutes into the talk, a group of women—students belonging to a group called Hopkins Feminists—stood up in protest. Dressed all in black, with duct tape over their mouths, they held up a sign and marched out of the hall.

YOU ARE RAPE CULTURE, the sign read.

Afterward, a reporter for the student paper asked Dershowitz about Jeffrey Epstein and Epstein's victims. Wasn't it true that Dershowitz had implied that one of those victims was "asking for it?"

"I'm a defense attorney," Dershowitz replied. "I have an obligation under the Constitution to provide a full and zealous defense to my clients. If I have failed to do all the things you had just listed, I could be disbarred. I could be found incompetent as counsel."

He asked the reporter, "Would any defense lawyer not look on the websites, look on social networks, find out what the woman who was accusing my client was doing? We were able to disprove many of the charges, just like how I was able to disprove the charges against me. Falsely charging somebody with rape is a heinous thing to do. First of all, it creates horrors for the person who has been falsely accused. Second, it so hurts real rape victims because it makes it clear that some women lie for money. Our country, unlike others, requires that everybody be defended, and I'm going to continue to do that whether my clients are guilty or innocent. Let me tell you, most of my clients have been guilty. They deserve a zealous defense just as anybody else. I'm very proud of what I did for Jeffrey Epstein. If people don't like the fact that I got a 'good deal,' that's the job I do."

The suits and countersuits Paul Cassell, Bradley Edwards, and Dershowitz filed against each other dragged on into the spring of 2016—reaching a crescendo with Dershowitz's argument about the plot to blackmail Les Wexner. But on April 8, all the parties involved agreed to settle, issuing a joint statement that read: "Edwards and Cassell acknowledge that it was a mistake to have filed sexual misconduct accusations against Dershowitz; and the sexual misconduct accusations made in all public filings (including all exhibits) are hereby withdrawn. Dershowitz also withdraws his accusations that Edwards and Cassell acted unethically. Neither Edwards, Cassell, nor Dershowitz have any intention of repeating the allegations against one another." Dershowitz also hired former FBI director Louis J. Freeh to do an independent investigation. Freeh concluded that the evidence his team reviewed refuted the accusations of sexual misconduct against Dershowitz.

For Alan Dershowitz, the long nightmare he'd had to endure as a result of his friendship with Jeffrey Epstein finally seemed to be over.

Ghislaine Maxwell

Trying to put her troubles with Epstein behind her, Ghislaine Maxwell took up a new calling.

"She's doing something to save the oceans now," a socialite says over the din of cocktail-party chatter at a private Palm Beach Club.

Maxwell's nonprofit, the TerraMar Project, describes itself as "a platform for citizenship and transformation of the high seas." Its focus is on cleaning up the eight million metric tons of plastic debris—garbage—that are dumped into the world's oceans each year. (Sources say that an earlier enterprise, the Seed Media Group, was funded by Jeffrey Epstein in 2005 to the tune of two million dollars.)

"Is anybody here staying awake at night because they're frightened about the ocean?" she asks in 2014 at a TEDx talk in Charlottesville, Virginia. "Are you scared about what could happen? Are you trying to think about what could you do that would help the ocean and all its myriad of troubles?"

But although her efforts on behalf of the environment are sincere and articulate, Ghislaine still appears in the society pages.

In 2010, she attends Chelsea Clinton's wedding in Rhinebeck, New York.

In 2014, New York journalist Richard Johnson reports that she's newly back from running in an Iditarod dogsled race in Alaska. "It's hard to top Ghislaine Maxwell in the globe-trotting department," he writes.

Upon her return, the president of the China Arts Foundation International hosts Maxwell at a dinner cooked by the former chef for Madame Chiang Kaishek.

Sources say that Maxwell still maintains her warm relationship with the Clintons. She was never charged with a crime. And Maxwell has repeatedly denied all allegations made by Virginia Roberts—and continues to do so today. Through her lawyer, Maxwell says she's had no connection to any criminal misconduct involving Virginia Roberts (or any other young woman) and Jeffrey Epstein. She claims that Virginia's story about her experience as a "sex slave" has changed, significantly, over time—that with each telling, Virginia adds salacious details and names new public figures. Nevertheless, legal troubles for Maxwell recently began.

In 2015, Virginia Roberts filed a defamation suit against the woman she says recruited her to work at Epstein's house on El Brillo Way. In January of 2016, Roberts filed additional papers, claiming that a defamation suit filed against Bill Cosby, another alleged sexual predator, was directly relevant to her case against Maxwell. In March, Maxwell filed an answer in court denying all of Roberts's allegations and accusing Roberts of fabricating them for financial gain.

As of this writing, the suit is ongoing.

Prince Andrew

In January of 2016, Sunninghill Park—the twelve-bedroom estate that Sarah Ferguson and Prince Andrew once shared in the English county of Berkshire—was bulldozed.

Prince Andrew had long since sold the home, which

he and Sarah had received as a gift after their 1986 wedding. He got into hot water when it was revealed that the buyer, a Kazakh billionaire named Timur Kulibayev, had paid three million pounds more than the home's asking price.

For her part, Sarah Ferguson announced that she was moving into a thirteen-million-pound ski chalet in Switzerland.

It was a fitting end to the long, sometimes sordid story of the prince's marriage. But it was not the end of the scandals that seemed always to be swirling around the prince.

On January 2, 2015, Virginia Roberts's allegations about her relationship with the prince—and the photo of him with his arm around Roberts's waist—appeared in the press. Prince Andrew was forced to cut short a skiing holiday to confer with his mother, the queen, and to issue a statement denying Roberts's allegations—a step that was widely seen as being without precedent for a member of the royal family.

That same month, at the World Economic Forum in Davos, Switzerland, the prince was again forced to "reiterate and to reaffirm" the repeated denials made by Buckingham Palace that he had any sort of sexual relationship with Roberts, who had announced in papers filed at the start of the year that Prince Andrew has a "sexual interest in feet."

"My focus is on my work," Prince Andrew said at the time.

Asked by a reporter, "Will you be making a statement?" the prince refused to answer.

A few days later, Virginia Roberts signed a sworn statement in which she said, "I did have sexual contact with him as I have described here—under oath. Given what he knows and has seen, I was hoping that he would simply voluntarily tell the truth about everything. I hope my attorneys can interview Prince Andrew under oath about the contacts and that he will tell the truth."

According to several reports, Roberts's lawyers had written to the prince, asking him to respond to her allegations in court. Reportedly, Buckingham Palace refused delivery of the letter.

"I knew he was a member of the British royal family, but I just called him 'Andy,'" Roberts had said in her statement. "I got news from Maxwell that I would be meeting a prince. Later that day, Epstein told me I was meeting a 'major prince.' Epstein told me 'to exceed' everything I had been taught. He emphasized that whatever Prince Andrew wanted, I was to make sure he got."

Signing her name to the document, Roberts wrote, "I declare under penalty of perjury that the foregoing is true and correct."

That spring, Prince Andrew got a rare break: a federal judge in South Florida ordered that the allegations Roberts made be stricken from civil-court records. "At this juncture in the proceedings, these lurid details are unnecessary," the judge concluded. Once again, Buckingham Palace vehemently denied the prince's involvement in any activities, sexual or otherwise, pertaining to Roberts. But that same year, reports leaked that the BBC program *Panorama* was working on an in-depth investigation into the prince's dealings with Epstein and Roberts.

As of this writing, the investigation has yet to air.

Barry Krischer

"I have no intention of being dragged into that conversation," Barry Krischer said in 2016 when contacted via telephone and asked about Jeffrey Epstein.

More than a decade had passed since Epstein's case first landed on the state attorney's desk.

"The *New York Times* has called me," said Krischer. "The British papers. I'm not interested in being pulled into that conversation. I know that the police chief didn't think the case was handled right, but that's why he's a cop and I'm a prosecutor."

Krischer, who left the state attorney's office in 2009, is still a member of the Criminal Justice Commission in Palm Beach County. Since his retirement, he's volunteered one morning a week at the office of the state attorney and two mornings a week at the Palm Beach County Sheriff's Office.

He still remains active in child welfare issues, working with the Florida Department of Children and Families.

Despite his continued involvement with local law enforcement, he hasn't spoken to Michael Reiter in years.

Bradley Edwards

In December of 2009, Jeffrey Epstein filed suit, under Florida's RICO act, against Scott Rothstein, the jailed Ponzi king; Bradley Edwards, the lawyer who'd worked, briefly, in Rothstein's law firm, RRA, and represented several of Epstein's victims; and one of those victims, an individual referred to in the lawsuit as "L.M."

"Upon information and belief," the suit stated, "EDWARDS knew or should have known that ROTHSTEIN was utilizing RRA as a front for the massive Ponzi scheme and/or were selling an alleged interest or investment in the Civil Actions (and other claims) involving Epstein." The suit also claimed that, "By using Civil Actions against EPSTEIN as 'bait' and fabricating settlements regarding same, ROTHSTEIN and others were able to lure investors into ROTHSTEIN'S lair and bilked them of millions of dollars which, in turn, was used to fund the litigation against EPSTEIN for the sole purpose of continuing the massive Ponzi scheme."

Moreover, the suit claimed, L.M. had "testified she never had sex with Epstein; worked at numerous strip clubs; is an admitted prostitute and call girl; has a history of illegal drug use (pot, painkillers, Xanax, Ecstasy); and continually asserted the 5th Amendment during her depositions in order to avoid answering relevant but problem questions for her." (The suit made similar claims about two other victims.) According to the suit, L.M. had said only good things about Epstein when interviewed by the FBI in 2007, while being represented by another lawyer. Her story "changed dramatically," the suit claimed, once she was "in the hands of EDWARDS and RRA."

In a motion for summary judgment filed by Bradley Edwards, Edwards denied all of these allegations, calling Epstein's claims frivolous for two separate reasons: On the one hand, Edwards claimed, Epstein was seeking damages from Edwards while asserting his own Fifth Amendment privilege to block the discovery of relevant facts. (And, in fact, Epstein did plead the Fifth, dozens of times, when deposed by the lawyers of his victims.) On the other hand, Epstein's claims were "directly contradicted by all of the record evidence.

"The truth in the record is entirely devoid of any evidence to support Epstein's claims and is completely and consistently corroborative of Edwards's sworn assertion of innocence," the motion stated.

Put simply, Epstein has made allegations that have no basis in fact. To the contrary, his lawsuit was merely a desperate measure by a serial pedophile to prevent being held accountable for repeatedly sexually abusing minor females. Epstein's ulterior motives in filing and prosecuting this lawsuit are blatantly obvious. Epstein's behavior is another clear demonstration that he feels he lives above the law and that because of his wealth he can manipulate the system and pay for lawyers to do his dirty work—even to the extent of having them assert baseless claims against other members of the Florida Bar. Epstein's Complaint against Edwards and LM is nothing short of a far-fetched fictional fairy-tale with absolutely no evidence whatsoever to support his preposterous claims. It was his last ditch effort to escape the public disclosure by Edwards and his clients of the nature, extent, and sordid details of his life as a serial child molester. Edwards's Motion for Summary Judgment should be granted without equivocation.

Edwards filed a counterclaim for malicious prosecution. "He sued me with knowingly made up, falsified facts," Edwards says.

And his sole motivation was to extort me into abandoning the legitimate cases I was pursuing against him on behalf of the victims, including the CVRA suit. He ultimately had to dismiss that case, literally on the morning our Summary Judgment was to be heard. I then sued him. We were set for trial. The judge granted me punitive damages in my claim. And then, in a separate case in Florida, one of the appellate courts basically abolished the tort of malicious prosecution in Florida. My case was dismissed. I then appealed that. And our district ruled that my malicious prosecution claim can stand and the tort is not abolished in Florida. They sent it back to the trial court and Jeffrey Epstein appealed that to the State Supreme Court, and that's where that stands.

Sarah Kellen

"She said her name was Clara something on the rental application," says a real estate agent in Palm Beach. "It wasn't until much later that I realized she was associated with Epstein."

In April of 2009, that agent rented Clara a bungalow in Palm Beach. For Clara, that little home was a step down from Jeffrey Epstein's big house on El Brillo Way and from the life she'd known as Sarah Kellen. But not *such* a step down. "She signed a lease to pay four thousand dollars a month from April 18 through July 18, 2009," says a Palm Beach resident familiar with the local housing market. "But she stayed a lot longer. And by the way, she went on a round-the-world trip for at least a month while she had the lease."

Kellen had been a prime suspect in Chief Reiter's investigation. Prosecutors had considered charging her, Wendy Dobbs, and Nadia Marcinkova as potential coconspirators. They'd avoided those charges as part of the plea deal that Epstein had struck—a deal in the course of which it was suggested that if Epstein had to have pleaded to *something,* he could have pleaded to striking Kellen—or slapping her, once, on his jet. Assault, they'd have called it.

Kellen might have gone along with that. But in the end she didn't need to. Sources say she found another rich man as Epstein whiled away his hours in and out of the Palm Beach Stockade. She reinvented herself, and when her relationship with the wealthy man fell apart, she played the field until she met and married a race-car driver named Brian Vickers. Along the way she reinvented herself yet again, changing her name to Sarah Kensington.

Nadia Marcinkova

Nadia Marcinkova changed her surname to Marcinko and, after training at a Palm Beach flight school, became a commercial pilot and certified flight instructor. Calling herself Gulfstream Girl on Facebook, she cultivated her social media presence until 2013, when the Gulfstream company filed a trademark infringement lawsuit against her. When the suit was settled out of court, in 2014, Marcinko changed "Gulfstream" to "Global."

"As a child," she wrote for the "About Me" page on her website, "Nadia channeled her entrepreneurial spirit by selling invisible pets to neighboring kids. She continued on to manage a successful family marketing business and soon she was discovered by a modeling agency and immersed into the marketing and advertising world as a spokesperson and international fashion model."

There is no mention of Jeffrey Epstein. But on her YouTube channel, Marcinko appears in the cockpit of a Gulfstream II that looks very much like Epstein's Gulfstream, sitting beside a man who looks much like Larry Visoski, a pilot for Epstein.

Marcinko's Manhattan address belongs to a building where Jeffrey Epstein's brother, Mark, owns the majority of apartments.

Sarah Kensington uses the same address in New York.

The Girls

One of the girls who gave Jeffrey Epstein massages moved to Los Angeles and became an actress, starring for a time in a soap opera and appearing in several films. She is now pursuing a career in country music.

Several girls have been arrested for drugs, prostitution, and other nonviolent crimes.

One girl is dead—murdered by her boyfriend for reasons that had nothing to do with Epstein.

One of the girls who claimed to have been raped by Epstein is now a successful real estate broker in South Florida.

Mary moved back in with her parents, finished high school, and attended college for a while. She had her ups and downs along the way. In 2010, she was arrested for shoplifting. But Mary, who was born in 1990, is still in her midtwenties—*still* young for a man of Jeffrey Epstein's age—with many good years ahead of her.

Wendy Dobbs studied nursing in college and became a bartender and waitress. "I want to fill a position in which I can [utilize] my communication and customer service skills to help others," she wrote on LinkedIn. "I feel I am at my best when I can make a difference in someone's life. My goal is to inspire and encourage others to make positive changes daily. If you are not reaching for the stars then your dreams are not big enough."

The Cops

Michele Pagan is now a sergeant for the Palm Beach Police Department.

In early 2012, at a reception at Mar-a-Lago, Detective Joe Recarey received the first Palm Beach Police Foundation Police Officer of the Year award—one of several honors he received in the course of his twenty-three-year career in Palm Beach. Two years later, he left the department and took a job as director of loss prevention for the Gold Coast Beverage company.

"I've been [at the Palm Beach Police Department]

longer than my children have been alive," he told a reporter for the *Palm Beach Daily News* when he left. "I'm going to miss a majority of the people I've worked with, and, obviously, I'm going to miss the work. This is my extended family. Like many families, you have disagreements with some family members. But you overlook that, and you work together and you're a team. I'm going to look back and miss a lot of the people I've worked with."

Palm Beach police chief Michael Reiter left the department in 2008 after twenty-eight years on the job. He now runs his own security company in Palm Beach.

Jean-Luc Brunel

In January of 2015, Jean-Luc Brunel sued his old friend Jeffrey Epstein, claiming that Epstein's fall from grace had cost him millions of dollars in business and caused him "severe emotional stress."

The lawsuit claimed, "Plaintiff Brunel is emotionally destroyed as a result of Epstein's actions and the resulting effects on his business. He has been on medications to deal with the effects of this."

It continues: "Defendant Epstein recklessly inflicted emotional distress on Plaintiff Brunel by engaging in illegal conduct with under-aged girls, which was falsely linked to Plaintiff.... This illegal conduct was extreme and outrageous by any standard."

The suit went on to quote Brunel's doctor, who said that the modeling scout had gone into psychotherapy "due to a subjective sense of depression related to what he believes is a loss of business in his modeling agency as a result of slander published against his business." Brunel had gone on prescription drugs—Prozac, Rivotril—as a result.

The fashion world had frozen him out, he said, after

his relationship with Jeffrey Epstein had become public. It had become impossible for him to find the "fresh
faces" he needed for his agency, MC2.

Brunel acknowledged Epstein's alleged crimes but
denied his own involvement. "Epstein's illegal activities
were outrageous and extreme; they involved receiving
massages from the under-aged girls while the girls were
nude or nearly nude; penetration of the girls with a finger or object; or full intercourse."

When the *Daily Beast* reported the story and reached
out to Brunel for a comment, the website's reporter was
told, "Jean-Luc is not in town; he's in South America."

Brunel's agency, MC2, is still in business.

Jeffrey Epstein

As of this writing, Jeffrey Epstein continues to entertain
young women at his Manhattan town house.

EPILOGUE

When John Connolly, Tim Malloy, and I began work on this book, I had hoped to interview Jeffrey Epstein myself: to look directly into the eyes of the man we'd be writing about. Epstein declined to sit for an interview. Many of his friends and associates did speak with us on the condition that they not be quoted. Several of them still liked Epstein and made a point of telling us what a loyal friend he was—although, like Icarus, he seemed to have a fatal flaw.

If Epstein had agreed to an interview, these are the questions I would have asked him:

- You pleaded guilty to a single felony count of soliciting prostitution from a minor. Do you believe in your heart that you were guilty?
- In 2011 you told the *New York Post*, "I'm not a sexual predator, I'm an 'offender.' It's the difference between a murderer and a person who steals a bagel." Do you stand by that statement today?
- Do you feel you were treated fairly by the criminal justice system?

- What effect did your conviction have on your business?
- Do you believe that you've done psychological harm to the women—especially the underage girls—you've been involved with?
- Are you still in touch with Ghislaine Maxwell?
- Are you in touch with Prince Andrew?
- You've spent time with Bill Clinton as well as Donald Trump. How would you characterize the two men?
- Several people have described you as a very loyal friend. Is that a fair characterization?
- I've heard that Leslie Wexner removed all photographs of you from his home. Given how close you once were, have you reconciled or tried to repair the relationship?
- Did the thirteen months you spent in jail change you in any way?
- After your stay in prison, have you continued to seek the company of very underage women?
- You were ordered to undergo psychological treatment as part of your sentence. Are you under treatment today?
- Do you regard yourself as having a sex addiction, and, if so, have you been treated for it?
- What is your greatest regret?
- What do you look for in a woman?
- Last question. How well do you sleep at night?

ABOUT THE AUTHORS

James Patterson is the world's bestselling author and most trusted storyteller. He has created many enduring fictional characters and series, including Alex Cross, the Women's Murder Club, Michael Bennett, Maximum Ride, Middle School, and I Funny. Among his notable literary collaborations are *The President Is Missing*, with President Bill Clinton, and the Max Einstein series, produced in partnership with the Albert Einstein estate. Patterson's writing career is characterized by a single mission: to prove that there is no such thing as a person who "doesn't like to read," only people who haven't found the right book. He's given over three million books to schoolkids and the military, donated more than seventy million dollars to support education, and endowed over five thousand college scholarships for teachers. The National Book Foundation recently presented Patterson with the Literarian Award for Outstanding Service to the American Literary Community, and he is also the recipient of an Edgar Award and six Emmy Awards. He lives in Florida with his family.

John Connolly has been an investigative reporter for twenty-five years, the last twelve of them with *Vanity Fair*. He has written scores of nonfiction pieces for numerous national magazines.

Tim Malloy is a thirty-year veteran of print and television journalism. He has won eight Emmys as an investigative reporter, documentary maker, and war correspondent. He appears in print, on the Web, and on TV as a political analyst.

For a complete list of books by

JAMES PATTERSON

VISIT
JamesPatterson.com

Follow James Patterson on Facebook
@JamesPatterson

Follow James Patterson on Twitter
@JP_Books

Follow James Patterson on Instagram
@jamespattersonbooks